Name _____

Address _____

R℞ PRESCRIBING REAL ESTATE

A DOCTOR'S GUIDE TO COMMERCIAL REAL ESTATE

Refills _____

M.D *Dr. Masaki Oishi, M.D, Ph.D.*

THE BENEFITS OF PASSIVE COMMERCIAL REAL ESTATE INVESTING

Dr. Masaki Oishi, MD, Ph.D.

MarketSpace.Capital
9100 Southwest Fwy
Suite 201
Houston, TX 77074

ISBN 978-0-578-84760-3

Printed in the United States of America

FOREWORD

In life, we encounter people whom we consider our friends, allies, and confidants. We meet people who are our teachers, educators and advisors, and we meet people who are our adversaries, our enemies, and our tormentors.

But the people whom we meet, even for a fleeting moment, that we will never forget are those people that influence, mold, and help shape who we are.

My influencer, and the man who gave me my first job, is Dr. W. Jost Michelson, MD. Dr. Michelson was the Chairman of Neurosurgery at Albert Einstein College of Medicine, that fine institution of higher learning that educated me and made me the neurosurgeon I am now.

Even today, some 20+ years later, I will never forget what Dr. Michelson taught me as a young student. So, if there is anything that you take away from this book, any wisdom at all, it should be these five, all important rules. They not only apply to neurosurgery, but they apply as a life lesson ... enjoy!

The Five Rules of Michelson

1. If whatever you are doing is working ... KEEP doing it;

2. If whatever you are doing is not working ... STOP doing it;

3. If you don't know what to do ... DO NOTHING;

4. It is easier to STAY out of trouble ... than to GET out of trouble; and

5. Never miss a good opportunity to SHUT UP.

DEDICATION

"Doctors need to go into practice with the end in mind."

Chandler George

You may be asking, "Who is Chandler George?"

Chandler George is one of the preeminent authorities on creating a "work-life balance." He has authored numerous publications, is a licensed chiropractor, the CEO, Chairman and owner of numerous med-spas and clinics, and has more than 20 years of experience in the field of Internet marketing.

But enough about Chandler George ... let's talk about you!

How can you—a successful physician with countless demands from patients, employees, physician groups, insurance companies, medical boards, family, health and wellness, bills to pay, etc.— create that work-life balance? How can you create the financial independence, wealth and prosperity that has been your lifelong dream? How can you do all of this without dedicating 15-hours a day, working multiple jobs, working a side-hustle, offering additional products, services, and treatments?

This book is dedicated to all the hustlers and your lifelong desire to achieve financial freedom, economic independence, and the ability to create substantial wealth while maintaining a satisfactory work-life balance.

All the best!

Dr. Masaki Oishi, MD, Ph.D.

CONTENTS

INTRODUCTION

My name is Dr. Masaki Oishi, but my friends call me "Mas." I am a trained neurosurgeon with decades of experience. However, I also have a passion for real estate. In fact, some say that I am "a practicing real estate developer by day, and licensed neurosurgeon by night!"

In addition to years of education, training, making rounds, and the never-ending practice of medicine, I am also the Co-Founder & Chairman of MarketSpace Capital, LLC, a private equity real estate firm that focuses on providing our valued capital partners with commercial real estate investment opportunities that generate consistent returns.

My desire in writing this book is to help other medical professionals get started with commercial real estate investing; a field I have been involved in for over 35 years, ever since I was 15 years old. So far, I have managed to amass a real estate investment portfolio of over $250 million in assets by working with our investors and co-development partners.

As a medical professional, I can relate to your current financial standing:

- You've managed to work your way into your current, high net-worth position(s) in your field of practice and are earning "good money." Getting here was not easy, but you did it. And that's appropriate because *our profession happens to be among the highest paying in the world.*

- Like me, in your earlier years, you probably assumed that all you had to do was work hard each day, climb that proverbial ladder of success to a high-paying career, at which point all your financial problems and "tales of woe" would be over. You constantly dreamed that you would make millions of dollars and retire extremely wealthy on your 120-foot yacht in a seaside resort somewhere in the south of France, along the French Riviera. It has been years now, and you have put in the countless hours, but *you are not yet that millionaire, your retirement expectations have now dramatically changed*, and the horizon for retiring with a sailboat in the Mediterranean still seems far away!

- As medical practitioners, many of us practicing in this industry see a six-figure income. However, such an income also places you in one of the highest tax brackets in the country. It is not unusual to end up paying 30-35 percent of your adjusted gross income in tax. With such a heavy tax burden, and the normal and customary expenses of daily life, *accumulating wealth becomes a seemingly far-fetched and uphill struggle.*

- What's more, and as you've probably already learned, having a lot of money parked in a bank account is not an effective wealth-building strategy; thanks to inflation, cash tends to lose its value over time. Just do the math: Your average 5-year certificate of deposit today pays a whopping 0.4 percent return, yet inflation over the past 5 years has averaged 3.24 percent—each and every year. You do not need a calculator to figure *out that your cash returns do not go near as far as they once did.* All it takes is a few decades, and all that hard-earned money will not be worth much to you.

- More disturbingly, cash and near-cash investments usually make it easier to spend money; not to mention the retirement of your large student debt from medical school, which is perhaps why doctors *rank as the largest industry group of high-income earning professionals, yet who are not millionaires.*

Think about it for a minute ...

If you have hundreds of thousands in the bank, would you not be tempted to buy that expensive car or boat? You may even try to convince yourself that ... "after all, these are not expenses - they are great fixed assets that will NEVER decline in value." And you continue to tell yourself that "since you've worked hard for it, isn't it only fair to reward yourself for all the insane hours you put in at work, not to mention school?"

The unfortunate truth is that income is not the same thing as wealth. The famed Dr. Thomas J. Stanley, author of The Millionaire Next Door, perhaps put it best when he said:

> *"If you make a six-figure income each year and spend it all, you are not getting wealthier; you are just living high. Wealth is what you keep."*

Keeping your money and using it to build wealth boils down to purchasing investments that tend to hold their value, exceed the levels of inflation, and appreciate over time. Real estate is one such investment.

Right about now as you are reading this introduction you are probably saying; *"Wow ... Mas, you have just described me and everything that has gone on in my financial life. But I am a doctor! I don't have time to devote to real estate investing. I work sixteen hours a day. When am I going to get the time or energy to manage real estate construction, working with architects, engineers, suppliers, quibbling over prices, cutting people down to the bone, and all that stuff?"*

Well, my friend, keep reading!

To invest in commercial real estate, you do not have to quit your day job to accomplish all of these ever-important tasks. Modern real estate investing is very flexible. Sure, you can make it your job to go out there and aggressively shop for bargains if you desire, or you can approach this exciting and lucrative venture in a more passive capacity that saves you time and headaches.

Here's something you should consider.

With your six-figure income level, your money could be earning you tens, perhaps hundreds of thousands of dollars each year in returns, without you having to invest a lot of time, effort, or energy.

I—and others like you and me—have invested successfully and have attained a great deal of financial independence and freedom. I did this without giving up my career as a neurosurgeon. I love being a neurosurgeon! It is my purpose, not just as a physician, but as a servant to the community-at-large to help my fellow man. There is no way that I will ever leave my practice or profession to become a "real estate guy." Equally important: There is no reason why you can't maintain your practice and invest in real estate.

The truth is that when you approach real estate as a passive investment, it can end up feeling like you are playing a game. You have certain decision to make—you follow the specific rules of the game—and as you go around the game board, you continue to accumulate an ever-increasing investment portfolio.

However, do not let the simplicity of this analogy delude you into thinking that real estate investing is easy; it is not, and it involves risks just like any other investment opportunity.

Making money in real estate, or anywhere else for that matter, is never going to be automatic. You need to have a firm grasp of what you are doing; and most importantly, you need to surround yourself with proven industry leaders who have successfully maneuvered around the potholes that life can sometimes throw in your path.

The purpose of this book is to help you navigate the rough-and-sometimes-rocky real estate investing waters using the systematic approach I have used to invest safely and successfully in commercial real estate over the past 35+ years. In short, learn from my mistakes, successes, and real-life educational experiences as you venture into the game-changing world of commercial real estate investing.

My systematic commercial real estate investing blueprint has served me well in the past, and continues to do so; even today as we face continued economic, social and healthcare uncertainties due to a worldwide pandemic. This blueprint is the same proprietary approach that my company, MarketSpace Capital, relies on when sourcing, researching, performing due diligence, structuring and eventually acquiring our target real estate investment opportunities.

If you want to succeed at acquiring, owning and operating a passive real estate investment portfolio, it really helps to have a systematic approach that allows you to make critical and well-informed decisions in a timely manner. You cannot leave your investment decisions to mere chance; in the same way that you cannot leave the health and safety decisions of your patients to mere chance. This book outlines, describes and shares the approach I use when investing in real estate.

If you trust the process, implementation strategies and investment recommendations that you learn from this book, you will not have to worry about contractors, material costs, capital structure, city codes, entitlements, regulations, and other such very important issues. You can simply invest and then get back to doing what you love doing the most—using your God-given skills and practicing medicine to enhance people's health and well-being.

Can it ever get any better than that?

In the chapters to come, I will introduce you to everything you need to know about investing in real estate, including:

- Why is commercial real estate such a good investment?
- What are the factors that make up the value of commercial real estate?
- How can I mitigate the investment risks of commercial real estate?
- How can I maximize the after-tax benefits of commercial real estate?
- How can I navigate the different types of commercial real estate?
- How can I use the current laws to best structure investments?
- What changes are coming through innovation and technology?

- How can I best capitalize on the market and economic cycles?

- And much, much more.

After you read this book, it is my hope that you have a prescription that includes the tools, knowledge, and confidence to purchase your first commercial real estate property. With time, and the ability to follow these investment recommendations, I am confident that you will start to grow and accumulate the wealth, prosperity and a work-life balance that has been your lifelong dream.

With all that said ... let's get started!

Name _____

Address _____

R ℞   CHAPTER ONE

WHY REAL ESTATE INVESTING?

Refills _____

M.D _____

"Ninety percent of all millionaires become so through owning real estate. More money has been made in real estate than in all industrial investments combined. The wise young man or wage earner of today invests his money in real estate."

Andrew Carnegie, billionaire industrialist

"I don't invest in cars, antiques, art or collectibles as that is merely a hobby and does not bring me a sense of happiness. Yes, I do have investments in stocks, commodities and bonds, but for the little (non-institutional) guy like me, I feel like I am always playing at a disadvantage. Larger investors with wealth managers and investment bankers have access to far more information and investment opportunities that are not available to regular investors like me. A lot of investment banks offer the illusion of equal opportunity, but that is a dangerous illusion.

As an equity investor, you must be smart, well diversified and strategic. Otherwise, you might as well take a trip to Las Vegas."

Dr. Masaki Oishi, Real Estate Investor

Let's start from the beginning:

- Why real estate?

- Why not something else?

- Why not something as exciting as stocks?

- Why not purchase shares in a startup and ride the wave to the top?

You've probably heard of individuals who have made fortunes this way.

Consider this: If you bought Apple stock in the early 2000s and reinvested the gains each year, a $1000 investment would be a cool $118,000 as of this writing.

While writing for CNBC's Make it, financial reporter Anna Hecht estimates that $1,000 invested in Amazon in 2009 would be worth $13,300 ten years later. These are excellent returns. These are certainly more compelling returns than, say, 30 percent a year in a shopping complex downtown.

Why, then, should you own a boring real estate investment that delivers "typical" returns when the goal is to become fabulously rich? Shouldn't you pick a couple of good stocks and hold them for the rest of your life?

First of all, consider that selecting high return stocks is no easy feat. Wall Street analysts earn six-figure salaries to do this kind of work. And I'm guessing you cannot afford to hire someone at such a ridiculous rate just to receive investment advice.

Second, the success rate in the stock picking game can be abysmally low. An estimated 95 percent of stock market speculators lose money. Unless you are a professional like the bankers at J.P Morgan, Goldman Sachs, or Merrill Lynch, the probability is high that you'll end up in the losing crowd. Remember, once you enter the game of equity investing, you're up against highly trained, educated and seasoned professionals who have faster performing equipment and more information. So ... good luck!

Third, many companies that go public eventually file for bankruptcy. A stock may look like a great buy right now, but a few years down the line, it may turn into a bad investment decision. There have been countless scary tales of companies that were once riding sky-high (think Enron), making investors happy. But today, they no longer exist. Remember, you may hold an investment that has good fundamentals, but something totally unrelated to your industry sector—such as a war, pandemic, terrorist strike, etc.—could force your equity values to zero.

Consider this fact: Of the original Dow Jones Industrial Average (DJIA) stocks, only General Electric is still there. The original Dow had major-league companies like American Tobacco and North American. They were typical blue-chip companies that virtually operated like monopolies and manufactured goods that seemed to be life-long commodities. You'd struggle to ever come up with safer bets on the stock market than these. Yes, they all went down!

I know what you're thinking, "Mas, get to the point already!"

Well, here it is: No matter how smart you think you may be at selecting good stocks, the chances of choosing a stock that will eventually go bankrupt are higher than your chances of selecting a stock that will ultimately earn you millions of dollars.

For most people, winning the stock picking game is a matter of luck, more than anything else. The people who win big and consistently in this game are those who stay well-diversified, or the professionals who know what they are doing and who work for hours a day to make their stock investing success a reality. Speculation in the stock market is no place for amateurs, and very seldom do you find the unicorn you are seeking.

I'm guessing you have no interest in betting your retirement money on just luck. After all, what did luck have to do with you going to medical school for years, finishing residency, getting an internship, and working impossible hours to earn millions throughout your career?

Simply stated ... Luck had nothing to do with it! Your success as a doctor resulted from hard work, determination, planning, perseverance, sacrifice, discipline, and, more importantly, patience. You didn't shortcut your way into being a valued member of the medical fraternity.

Likewise, thinking that you can buy some stock, forget about it, and sit back hoping to get rich someday, is about the craziest idea you can ever come up with, and you know better. Many wealthy people know this all too well, which is why an estimated 90 percent of millionaires worldwide own real estate. Stock market millionaires, on the other hand, are a minority among the very wealthy. Investors like Warren Buffet, Peter Lynch and others may get a great deal of media attention, but these are not passive investors. These are professionals supported by a team of hundreds of financial analysts, industry researchers, lawyers, accountants, operators, etc. In other words, these are hands-on, very active and dedicated investors.

Based on the numbers alone, it's perhaps best to say that real estate is quite frankly one of the safest investment options, at least when it comes to an investment that promises a decent rate of return.

Let's go beyond the numbers and talk more about why real estate investing is a good idea.

Why Real Estate Is the Best Long-Term Investment

Long-term, investing in real estate is better than all other strategic investment options because:

1: Real estate is a renewable source of capital

Owning real estate means you always have a capital source that, except for unusual cases of a down cycle, generally keeps adjusting upwards which can only be a good thing because growing your wealth means you can invest in other projects.

Many real estate investors borrow against the value of their existing property to fund more projects. This benefit is mostly unique to real estate, as margin requirements limit the amount of leverage available in equity securities.

But why is this possible in real estate?

First, you have to consider the appreciating nature of real estate properties. A property's value generally will rise, and often does so due to multiple factors such as inflation, growing rents and net operating income, supply and demand factors, and the ability to shelter income, thereby allowing investors to keep more net income after taxes.

For instance, if you purchase a property worth $1 million, its value might increase to $1.5 million in five years. At the same time, you've likely reduced your principal by paying off part of your mortgage. Thus, your equity holdings in the property increase.

At this point, the banks will most likely be interested in a mortgage refinance deal that allows you to lock in your gains and probably get better and more attractive mortgage terms such as a lower interest rate or longer amortization period. You can then borrow, using your new equity in the property as collateral to pursue other projects like constructing new buildings or expanding your real estate portfolio.

It is hard to pinpoint other investment options that allow you to leverage your existing holdings to acquire more credit.

2: Wealth creation

Every investor has one ultimate goal: wealth creation! If that's what you want too, real estate is your best bet.

The overall process is quite simple: If you acquire a rental property by putting up a small amount of money as your down payment equity (perhaps 20 percent), the bank puts up the remaining 80 percent of the purchase price. If conditions are right and the purchase price was appropriate, the rental property should provide net cash flow that pays for all mortgage expenses plus other miscellaneous costs like insurance, taxes, maintenance, etc. Meanwhile, the property's value appreciates.

Depending on the type of mortgage, you could pay off your mortgage in 15 to 30 years. Also, keep in mind the property's value will generally keep appreciating throughout the mortgage repayment period. At the end of it all, you are the rightful owner of a valuable piece of fully-paid off real estate whose value will have appreciated significantly over time.

This concept is so straightforward that we can summarize it into a simple formula:

principal reduction + property value appreciation = long-term wealth creation

To put this into context, let's look at an example.

Let's assume you've done your homework and have located an office building complex downtown worth $200,000. Typically, the bank expects you to pay 20 percent as a down payment.

In this example, your initial investment in the property is $40,000. To make things a bit easier, you have opted for a 25-year, fixed-rate mortgage of $160,000 at 4.5% interest.

The real estate market is doing well, and you are confident that the rental income from the property will cover all monthly expenses and still allow you $200 in free cash flow each month. In this example, just in your first year, you'll receive a $2,400 return on your $40,000 bet right off the bat. That is a 6% per annum current return! Not so bad, is it?

Here's something else you have to keep in mind: Each year, rent rates tend to go up by approximately 2 to 3 percent (say 2.5%), depending on inflation, supply and demand, etc. Even better, your property's value is likely to increase each year as a result of the expanding net cash flow.

Now, the exciting thing is that by year five, you will typically find that your equity has more than doubled (equity is the difference between the property's value and the mortgage balance you owe the banks).

If you're wondering why the value of your investment will increase that fast, it is because while your property's value will likely rise at a modest rate, the balance on your mortgage will be reduced because the rental income you are receiving monthly is practically paying for everything including the interest and principal on the mortgage.

The real game in real estate mostly lies in how quickly your equity in a property investment rises over time through mortgage reductions.

By year 30, you have paid off your mortgage, and your property's value has more than tripled to roughly $650,000. And the rental income is now at a record high because your expenses are not inclusive of mortgage payments.

Imagine a scenario where you have invested in several properties and that your plans followed pretty much the same hypothetical scenario we have discussed. By the time you retire, you could be fabulously wealthy.

The following is an example of this illustration, being supported by the numbers:

	Year 0	Year 1	Year 2	Year 3	Year 4	Year 5
Building Value	$ 200,000	$ 205,000	$ 210,125	$ 215,378	$ 220,763	$ 226,282
Down Payment	$ (40,000)					
Loan Balance	$ 160,000	$ 156,456	$ 152,748	$ 148,871	$ 144,815	$ 140,573
Net Cashflow		$ 2,400	$ 2,460	$ 2,522	$ 2,585	$ 2,649
Cash on Cash Return		6.0%	6.2%	6.3%	6.5%	6.6%
Equity	$ 40,000	$ 48,544	$ 57,377	$ 66,508	$ 75,948	$ 85,709

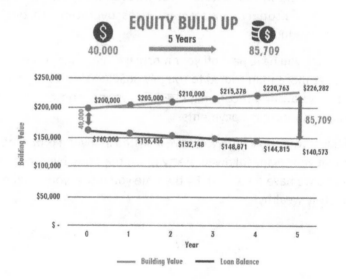

3: Increased cash flow

Another attractive benefit to real estate investing is that it can provide an ever-rising passive income.

Passive income is money earned without active involvement in a business venture. This form of income is attractive because it doesn't keep you from practicing medicine—the money keeps rolling in, even if you're sleeping. This is not to be confused with what my father told me as a kid, "Never invest in anything that eats while you sleep!" Therefore, investing in race horses, llamas and chinchilla farms is off limits.

As you probably already know, there are many ways of building a passive income source. Some people invest in automated businesses while others lease or license intellectual property, and still others create online businesses, and so on. These are all great strategies in their own right.

However, as a medical practitioner who is probably very busy helping people, it is vital that you choose investment options that don't demand too much active participation. In my experience, there are very few available passive income opportunities that allow your income to increase over time the way real estate does.

Rents generally go up to keep pace with inflation, and in particularly bullish economic times or because of other macro-economic and supply-and-demand factors, rental income can even double in a short time. You'll struggle to find such investment opportunities elsewhere.

4: Powerful and consistent growth

Every industry and investment is subject to market cycles, and as a passive investor, you want to own investments that can survive economic downturns without much volatility. Of course, real estate certainly fits that mold.

The stock market may attract aggressive investors looking to get rich quickly, but stocks or other equity investments usually take the brunt of bearish economic downturns. Sometimes equity investors end up losing everything during these unfortunate times.

If you look back to 2008, the DJIA fell 777 points in one day of intraday trading, undoubtedly one of the worst drops seen up to that point. Such a decline wiped out many peoples' wealth, and all the other major market averages saw significant decreases as well.

I'm not implying that real estate prices do not fall during such times, because they do; but the fall is generally not as dramatic as is the case with stocks.

All this highlights the fundamental strengths and weakness associated with highly liquid markets. They can be exciting to play because you can get in and out whenever you want and the transaction costs are also lower, but when things turn sour, they do so quickly and drastically with passive investors usually being the worst hit.

Keep in mind that, in liquid markets, computers equipped with high-frequency algorithms that can place trades and abort them in fractions of seconds rule the day. That is perhaps why price movements are highly erratic when the "herd mentality" takes effect.

If you are not in front of your screen most of the time, watching the performance of your portfolio, you could lose your investment in a very short period of time. Is that what you wish to do with your money? I would guess not!

In comparison, a real estate investment is a stable instrument. Values rise slowly but steadily. Rents rise slowly, but steadily. Mortgage debt is reduced slowly, but steadily. You can invest your money and still get a good night's sleep because you know you can survive and thrive despite short-term ups and downs.

5: Tax benefits

As a high-income earner, income tax could be your most significant expense, bigger even than any single household expense you might have. That is not a fun position to be in, especially when you consider how recklessly the government spends our tax dollars!

The good news is that real estate is practically the only investment vehicle that offers tax benefits unavailable in most other investment vehicles. It would be wise to take advantage of this because, presently, you are probably paying a huge amount of income tax on the money you are earning from your profession. If you invest in other opportunities that still require you to pay large amounts of tax, pretty soon you'll be paying far more tax than you should.

While you will have to consult with a tax accountant or attorney, as it turns out, depreciation, insurance, repairs, salaries, and other real estate associated expenses all offer opportunities to reduce your overall tax burden. The largest of these line items, depreciation, is a non-cash item and serves as a true shelter to offset your tax burden.

As long as you don't sell any of your holdings, you can usually postpone capital gains tax payments for as long as you want. Even if you do sell a property, there is a way to reinvest the proceeds in another property and still postpone tax payments. As stated before, you can even secure debt to refinance a portion of your equity out of the project, without the imposition or payment of any capital gains taxes. Where else can you get benefits like these?

6: Stays up with inflation

A safe investment is only as good as its ability to show returns that can beat inflation. That is one of the many reasons why saving your money in the bank is a bad investment approach for the long haul; your money sits there doing nothing, and the returns you get are not good enough to justify such idle potential.

Today, you will be lucky to earn a return that keeps up with inflation on a high-yield savings account, certificate of deposit, US Treasury, etc. Investopedia recently published a list of the best high-yield savings account: No bank on the list offers even 2 percent APY, let alone the current rates of inflation!

Inflation eats away at your money at a rate of roughly 3.24 percent each year, during the past 100 years. Thus, by putting your money in the bank, you will be falling behind each year and actually generating a negative return after the effects of inflation.

Compare that with the median rate of return on investment found in commercial real estate. Over the last 25 years, estimates show that this return has averaged 9.4 percent according to the National Council of Real Estate Investment Fiduciaries (NCREIF). While other investments may offer returns that rival real estate returns, their highly erratic performance is concerning. You simply cannot be confident that you will turn a profit on your holdings each year.

Right about now you are asking, "Mas, what's the bottom line?"

Here it is: If you want a passive investment that delivers healthy returns, protects your current living standard, and lets you keep more of what you earn, real estate is one of the safest and best bets for you.

7: Competitive advantage

It is often misunderstood, but you do not make money when you sell real estate; you actually make money in real estate when you acquire the property. You merely collect your earnings upon the sale, but you capture and lock in your profits at the original purchase! Consequently, making a deal at the right price is imperative.

Information is also important in real estate. Much of the time, as long as both parties agree on a price, a transaction can occur. It doesn't matter that the bargain is absurd and almost borders on being unfair. If someone is naïve and doesn't want to know much about real estate, someone more knowledgeable and experienced can take advantage of the situation.

The same thing can happen in markets like stocks, commodities, and other areas. The government has created policies, rules and regulations to protect the novice and uninformed investor from illegal trades in these industries using any material, non-public information. Benefiting from information that is not yet public knowledge is not acceptable. There is a name for it: it's called *insider trading*, a crime that's punishable by hefty fines—up to $5 million—and incarceration—up to 20 years.

In 2013, the Securities and Exchange Commission (SEC) fined SAC Capital Advisors, one of the biggest hedge funds participating in the capital markets, a record $1.8 billion, and ordered them out of business for being a market cheater that profited from knowledge not available to the general public.

Such occurrences are nearly unheard of in real estate. If you have enough knowledge and contacts, you can hear about and benefit from off-market transactions, confidential information or detailed entitlements regarding your neighboring properties—information that nobody else knows about, all the while operating within the confines of the law.

For instance, consider an area of real estate investing called Covered Land Play (CLP). It involves buying properties you intend to renovate or improve, driven by the goal of boosting your returns over the long-term. Real estate investors favor this approach because it presents an opportunity to achieve higher returns with limited downside risk.

Here's how it works: You purchase a property that is an existing income-producing property that already has positive cash flow, but that you and your development team know it can turn into something better and more beneficial to the surrounding community. The property's income stream should cover most of the cost associated with operating it during the renovation, thereby making it a cheaper, more efficient operation.

The main attraction to such a real estate project is its longer-term potential and is less about its current cash flow. In the short-term, the returns may be modest, but the returns are likely to be substantial in the long run.

To take advantage of CLPs, you usually need some knowledge that is not generally available.

For example, you will need to know things such as future developments planned in that area, the local government vision, local area market performance, and other things unknown to much of the public.

Having this type of information and acting on it will not get you in trouble with the law which would be the case if you were playing the stock market. The law considers having such information "a competitive advantage."

Now that you are conversant with all the primary reasons why real estate investing is better than most other forms of investment, let's talk about something else which is equally important ...

The Difference Between Active and Passive Real Estate Investors

All the various ways of making money in real estate can fall into two categories: *passive* and *active investing*. No matter what you do, you will fall under one of these categories.

Given this, you should be in a position to tell the difference, thereby ensuring you understand where you belong and why.

Let's talk about passive investing first.

1: Passive investing

Passive investing is a more relaxed making-money approach, usually not typified by active involvement. Here's how it works.

First, you do your homework, select your investment, purchase it, and then sit back, watching as the financial fun happens.

Passive investing is the sort of thing you want to get involved in, if you are busy doing something else—such as focusing on your medical practice. I know this because this approach is the essence of the blueprint I use to invest in the real estate market.

When I got involved in real estate, I performed my due diligence to understand the game as much as possible. I quickly learned that real estate goes deep, and only you can choose how deeply you want to get involved.

I love my career! My love for neurosurgery is one of the reasons I worked so hard for many years to get to where I am today. I am proud of it. I wasn't going to give it all up and go into real estate— yes, real estate can easily become your full-time job.

Because of my love for medicine, I made up my mind right away; I would work hard at my chosen career and use real estate as a passive investment tool. I didn't want to obsess over staying on top of market trends, planning my exit strategies, trying to time the market, or engage with a myriad of professionals at all times. That's the kind of thing that real estate professionals do, and we will talk about these people in just a bit.

Now, if you love being a doctor as much as I assume you do, I advise you to follow the passive investing approach as well—unless you want to quit your job as a doctor to pursue real estate full-time.

That brings me to one caveat you need to know regarding this approach: Adopting a completely hands-off approach to real estate, without involving seasoned professionals, means your returns will be slow and steady over time, but not as exciting as what consummate professionals who do all the hard work will get.

In essence, your primary source of wealth will be your career. Your real estate investments will be a way to store your wealth safely and allow it to grow slowly and steadily, in a way that more than keeps up with inflation.

You're probably wondering, "Mas, I want to become a passive real estate investor. How do I get started?"

There are two ways:

1. The first one is direct passive investing. With this option, you purchase a property (or a piece of it) and then hire a third party, such as a management company, to run it for you. They will collect rent, handle repairs, market and secure tenants, pay taxes on your behalf, and deposit your profits in your bank account.

2. The second approach is indirect passive investing. With this approach, you put your money in a trust company or fund involved in the real estate business. It's a little like purchasing an interest in a business, and a lot like buying into a mutual fund. If you find a reputable company with a good track record, they will handle all the grunt work and ensure that your money works for you while you tend to other things in your life. Your job will be to collect

dividends and enjoy increased value holdings. As a quick shameless plus, MarketSpace Capital is one such company.

I faced these exact decisions and questions as my portfolio was expanding, and so I decided to form MarketSpace Capital to accomplish the real estate investment allocation of my family office. At MarketSpace Capital, we strive to make the dream of investing in passive income-generating real estate a reality for medical professionals.

We help our clients and partners look at all the important facts regarding an investment in consideration. Once we are confident clients understand all the facets of an opportunity, we take care of the execution phase.

At MarketSpace Capital, we have a team of reliable and competent professionals on staff who will handle all the details regarding bringing any project to life that our investment committee approves.

2: Active investing

Active investing is the opposite of passive investing.

It refers to the active acquisition and management of an investment/asset.

To carry out active investing, you must be willing to do the hard work which makes this approach very intense and demanding. Many of the people you've heard of who have made real estate fortunes in a short period are active investors.

The extraordinary profits made by active investors mostly have to do with well-timed market entries and exits. To do that, you must know everything you possibly can about real estate and have excellent timing. And yes, being lucky also helps.

A perfect example is real estate speculation which is not terribly different from what happens in stocks, bonds, commodities and other liquid markets. You can buy something for cheap and sell it at a higher price in a short amount of time, and vice-versa.

It is not unusual to purchase a property at a bargain price and sell it a few months at a higher price and make a nice profit. Buy low, sell high is a winning formula. Even the opposite is possible: You can sell properties in a falling market, repurchase them at rock-bottom prices later, and profit from the difference.

The same level of activity is involved with things like real estate development, house flipping, and all manner of money-making strategies that require you to watch things carefully to prevent them from spinning out of control.

To do these kinds of things well, you have to know what you are doing. You have to stay on top of things at all times. That is why active investing can be a full-time job. I know of highly dedicated real estate investors who work round the clock for as much as 20 hours a day.

You probably have little taste for that kind of involvement, thus making active investing in real estate not a good fit for you.

The next question you might be having is, "Mas, what can I expect from passive investing in real estate?"

To answer that question, you first need to understand what we call the "preferred return," also called a hurdle rate. The hurdle rate is the minimum threshold of returns a fund or investment must achieve and pay to the capital investors, or limited partners, before the general partners can compensate themselves.

With most syndication and funds, including MarketSpace Capital, the annual preferred return is typically 8 percent. That means that the return on all invested funds must be at least 8 percent each year before we can start receiving our share of the profits, also called carried interest.

Let's look at an overly simplified example to illustrate the point.

Let's assume you have invested $100,000 in a fund, and at the end of the first year the property is sold and the profits that year are $50,000. You have also agreed to split the remaining profits equally with the general partner.

Therefore, if we assume the typical preferred return of 8 percent, $8,000 should first go into your pockets. That leaves $42,000 to be split between you and the general partner, meaning you will each receive $21,000 as compensation. Thus, overall, as the capital investor, you will end up receiving $29,000 in total, or a return on your investment of 29 percent per year!

To go back to your question ...

You can reasonably expect a minimum return of 8 percent if, yes, if everything works according to plan. You are also entitled to a proportional share of the excess profits.

If things don't go according to plan, and the investment falls short of the 8 percent threshold, all the profits will get paid to capital investors, while the general partner(s) get nothing. This structure, I feel, incentivizes our team at MarketSpace Capital to work hard so that returns are good enough to benefit both you and MarketSpace Capital in the long run.

You also have to consider that in some instances, particularly in a booming real estate market, the asset prices can appreciate, and all it takes is a refinancing transaction to pay back most, if not all of your invested capital.

Here's something else you also have to keep in mind ...

You are entitled to a proportional share of the profits from the sale of any particular asset the fund resorts to selling.

Let's take things a step further and bust some myths about real estate investing.

5-Common Myths About Commercial Real Estate Investing

Let's discuss five common myths concerning commercial real estate investing.

Myth #1: You need to have a lot of money or near-perfect credit to invest.

In reality, this is nowhere near the truth.

First, all banks truly care about is whether you can afford to make the down payment on a property. Usually, this figure amounts to 20 percent of the property's value. In other instances, depending on the bank's policy and the attractiveness of a deal, you might even have to put up less, such as a 10 percent down payment.

For example, if you want to invest in a deal involving a $200,000 property, a $40,000 down payment would be customary. With your level of income, this should be relatively attainable.

Even better, if you don't have a lot of money, you can purchase shares in a fund or syndicated trust. Even with such vehicles, you're still investing in commercial real estate, but you do not have to come up with a lot of money since you're pooling funds with other investors.

For instance, with most Real Estate Investment Trusts (REITs) that do not trade in the stock exchange yet, the minimum investment ranges from $1,000 to $2,500. You can certainly come up with money like that!

Second, in this instance, banks genuinely don't care much about your credit because the payments will be coming from the property, not from you. Banks care more about the project's viability and collateral values. All you have to do is make your case and convince them that the market and the project's income potential will be good enough for them to get involved.

That means creating as detailed a plan as possible and ensuring you document all the research that justifies your position.

Myth #2: Investing in real estate is a complicated full-time job.

Again, this is simply not true.

As discussed previously, real estate can only be a full-time job for those interested in becoming active investors. Otherwise, there are passive ways to approach real estate investing without having to lift a finger.

If you find that you have a very demanding career you love, you can purchase a property asset and find a real estate management company that can manage it for you. You also have the option of placing your money in a trust or a fund that has an excellent track record.

In both options, your money works for you, and you don't have to spend a lot of time and energy to get involved.

Myth #3: Real estate investing is too risky.

Life itself is risky, and practically every money-making opportunity involves risk. There is simply no way to avoid it completely. Even when you do not take financial risks, you automatically place yourself in a different kind of risky situation where you may not meet your future financial goals.

The key to successful risk-taking is to understand the involved risk and, to the best of your ability, control it, and use it to your advantage. When appropriately handled, risks do not and should not always imply a losing situation.

First, the reality that most real estate assets appreciate over time is reason enough to get involved without obsessing over risk. If real estate assets' historical value kept going down, it would be safe to assume that investing in real estate is very risky and, therefore, not wise. But that doesn't seem to be the case at all.

Second, the character of real estate markets is generally stable and not highly erratic. Variability in price fluctuations is a crucial indicator of risk: the more a financial instrument's value fluctuates up and down, the higher risk attached to the investment opportunity.

Stocks, as a rule, are characteristically very volatile. Even though the stock market generally appreciates in the long run and in the aggregate, the movement has characteristically treacherous ups and downs that can scare off most investors, especially those whose risk appetite is low.

Actually, one of the many reasons why most stock market investors lose money is because people panic and sell their holdings during short-term price corrections, thereby missing out on long-term gains.

In real estate, prices are much more stable, with the rise and fall being much smoother. Prices will generally not rise and fall overnight, causing you to lose sleep.

Therefore, real estate is a much better fit for investors who like to sleep well at night, or those looking for a more passive and limited involvement.

Myth #4: Good real estate deals are hard to come by.

If you are new to real estate, then finding deals on your own can certainly be difficult.

It may be difficult because you have limited knowledge of what you are doing and of the market. Another problem is that you may have no industry contacts whatsoever.

Does that mean it's all over? That there is no hope?

Heavens no!

Deals happen all the time in real estate. As you read this, countless deals are going to close by the end of the day.

The key to finding quick real estate deals is to start by working with established professionals. For instance, locate and talk to commercial real estate brokers. They have considerable firsthand knowledge and are like walking and talking information databases on market data and possible deals. After all, they only get paid if and when the transaction closes.

Real estate attorneys, tax advisors, and CPAs who have clients in the real estate business are also a good source for potential deal flow.

Things will only be difficult if you attempt to work alone. If you partner with other people, you will be amazed at how easy it is to locate deals. Moreover, as you work and establish contacts, you will gain an edge in finding future deals. This does not mean you should surrender your own judgment as to whether a deal makes sense for you, but it is a good place to get started.

Myth #5. If a property is for sale, then there must be something wrong with it.

In a way, this type of fear has some justification. At MarketSpace Capital, we sometimes encounter people who want to sell something so they can get out of trouble. They want to unload their problem onto someone else who has less knowledge—it happens all the time! After all, remember the wise saying: *Caveat Emptor* ... Let the buyer beware!

However, you should not let this fear paralyze you. Not all deals are bad. Quite a number of them are genuine. The only way to ease concerns regarding bad deals is to do your homework thoroughly.

Before you consider getting into a deal, first analyze all facts and figures. Ensure you are not overlooking any critical criteria, and when something checks out, it's likely a good thing.

Another thing you can do is to work with experienced professionals. Nothing can beat having an experienced professional as a personal advisor and having such a partner can save you from many bad deals. I can honestly say that I have never lost money on a deal I did not feel made sense for me. If it does not feel right or the due diligence starts to raise red flags, then walk away. Don't worry about offending people – this is business, and deals can fall through.

For example, let's assume you're considering the purchase of a specific office building in a particular area of town. You have gone through the due diligence checklist that MarketSpace Capital has provided and everything checks out, but something in your gut is making you feel unsure about the deal. You are not sure whether you should take the plunge. So you stew in confusion.

A quick way to solve this dilemma is to call and seek counsel from a commercial real estate agent you can trust. The consultation might cost you a bundle, but in the end, it may help you dodge money-draining pitfalls...

With the most prevalent myths covered, let's now discuss an important subject regarding an investment portfolio: diversification, something many investors often disregard.

Real Estate as a Method of Diversifying Your Investment Portfolio

Diversification is a way of reducing risk by allocating investment capital across a wide range of uncorrelated assets. For instance, you might allocate some capital to stocks and bonds, some to commodities and small businesses, some to treasury bills, etc.

Diversification is crucial because the underlying assumption is that one asset's gains will counterbalance losses in another asset class, thereby reducing the probability of a significant loss to your overall portfolio. This counterbalance is crucial, especially if you're a non-sophisticated, passive investor.

Real estate provides diversification opportunities because one independent asset class has low correlation with another asset class price movement and volatility.

How exactly might you employ diversification when it comes to real estate?

I recommend following the 20 percent rule, invented by David Swensen, Chief Investment Officer at Yale Endowment. According to Swensen, all investors should allocate at least 20 percent of their investment capital to alternative assets.

Alternative assets are investment opportunities that do not include intangibles like stocks, bonds, certificates, or cash. A good way to think about alternative investments is to think of precious metals, art, jewelry, and, you guessed it, real estate.

Even though you might have holdings in other asset classes, I recommend that you consider allocating about 20 percent of your portfolio into real estate. It will balance out things nicely, and you won't have to worry as much about market risk or losses.

Earlier, we mentioned how, like most other things, investing in real estate has an attendant level of risk. Let's talk about these risks for a moment.

The Risks of Investing in Real Estate (and How to Safeguard Against Them)

As mentioned, like most other investment opportunities, real estate investing has some risk—life itself is risky.

The primary risk attached to real estate investing is that there are no guarantees, but such is life. Besides this main risk, what other risks are there, and how can you safeguard your investment against value decline?

Let's look at some of them.

1: General market risk

General market risk refers to factors that will affect the real estate market as a whole, most of which are beyond your control. For instance, factors like the rise and fall of the general economy, fluctuating interest rates, recessions in correlated markets, natural disasters, and other market risks that are all outside your control.

The only way to guard against total annihilation by such risks is to hedge your bets. The best way to hedge is to diversify your portfolio holdings. Do not put all your investment eggs in the real estate basket. It's a foolhardy approach. It's advisable to invest just a portion of it.

I advised that 20 percent is good starting point, but you may consult your own professional financial advisor on what portion of your capital you should invest in an individual asset class in relation to your other holdings.

2: Asset-level risk

This risk has more to do with the sensitivity of consumer demand associated with a certain property type. The demand for certain properties is stable throughout a typical year. In stark contrast, the demand for other properties may be seasonal and erratic. Thus, properties that have stable demand all year have little risk. For instance, multifamily residential properties are usually in demand, even during bad economic times, making their risk significantly lower.

Office buildings may rank second on the sensitivity scale. Other properties like shopping malls, hotel resorts, and the like have a more elastic occupancy and are more sensitive and riskier.

Once again, diversification is the best way to minimize the probability of financial ruin posed by this type of risk.

3: Idiosyncratic risk

Idiosyncratic risk refers to risk peculiar to a particular property. If you think about it, you'll realize that many factors may contribute to the risk associated with a specific property.

Take location, for example. A property's location can be in a flood-prone area, making it less attractive to tenants. Also, a property can be in a neighborhood replete with gangs and violent criminals.

Another factor that contributes to idiosyncratic risk is construction. There are many variables when it comes to construction, and at times it can get pretty expensive and exceed the allocated budget. Before you know it, you are in a financial hole because of a particular project.

What if a construction worker gets severely injured or dies? Suddenly, you're facing substantial financial commitments than you had not bargained for at the start of the project.

In some instances, a project may grind to a halt because the government is dragging its feet before approval, and as time goes by your risk exposure increases.

4: Liquidity risk

Liquidity risk is another form of risk peculiar to real estate. Unlike many publicly-traded markets, liquidity in real estate is considerably lower.

Liquidity refers to the ease of entering and exiting a particular investment opportunity at a specific time and price point without incurring high costs. It is a direct function of the number of market participants at a particular time who are willing to take the other side of your transaction.

If the number of people participating in a particular market is high, buying or selling becomes easy. The opposite applies when there are fewer buyers and sellers with ready cash.

In real estate, lack of liquidity can work to your disadvantage, especially when you're exiting an investment. Finding buyers is not always easy, especially during market downturns, and most often it takes experienced brokers and real estate agents to find willing buyers during such times.

This situation can be incredibly disheartening; there is nothing worse than holding onto an investment that's hemorrhaging money every day, wishing you could find someone to unload it onto, but unable to do so.

That is not usually the case with liquid markets like stocks.

When a stock price falls, and you wish to exit, rest assured that you can almost always find a buyer willing to take the other side of the trade, especially if you are a small operator. With stocks, quick exits are possible—unless your holdings are massive and you're operating during times of low liquidity.

Even then, you usually have the benefit of holding a market up or down by taking an even larger position by "doubling down," then waiting for more favorable conditions to start dumping your positions.

In other instances, especially when working with retail brokers, the broker is usually willing to take the other side of your transaction when nobody else can. Even though you might end up incurring higher commission costs and spreads, it is usually a much better scenario than never getting the chance to get out as a bear market puts you through the wringer.

5: Credit risk

This type of risk has to do with the stability of cash-flows from a property, which usually has a lot to do with the tenants' financial stability and creditworthiness.

Typically, the more stable the cash-flow, the higher and more desirable a property is, and vice versa.

For instance, if a bank has rented the entire building, it is a much safer option for you than if several unestablished retail operators do so.

6: Replacement risk

What are the chances that someone will put up a better facility with more current features than your current property, and what will be the implications of such a development? Will the new developer charge rates comparable to yours? Will they even pose the risk of stealing all your tenants? What will be the cost of renovation? Will it justify the returns?

Replacement risk is a real issue you have to consider. An old, dilapidated building in a market filled with a sea of new construction buildings poses significant replacement risk, and you will have to weigh your options carefully before you get involved.

7: Leverage risk

Leverage simply means borrowing to invest. When you borrow money from a bank to finance the purchase or construction of a new building, you are leveraging.

Virtually everyone in real estate operates with leverage. It's just too risky and prohibitively expensive to go into a project with all your money tied up.

Now, as you get started, you should watch out for the amount of leverage you take on. A lot of leverage can magnify your returns, but it can also be risky. If you allow yourself to go in over your head with debt, you risk losing your initial investment and getting into an unending cycle of debt, which is a relatively easy trap to fall into when times are good.

One of the best ways to minimize your leverage risk is to have a maximum threshold for the amount of leverage you accept. A good rule is to take on 75 percent of your total purchase price in leverage as a safe threshold. In other words, on most deals, aim to put up at least 25 percent of your own cash equity, and let the bank put up the rest.

You don't want to find yourself in a situation where you are upside-down, with your equity having dwindled to a point where you owe more than your property's worth.

The benefits of investing in real estate usually far outweigh the risk. One of these benefits relates to taxes:

The Tax Benefits of Real Estate

I have hinted before at the idea of real estate offering a slew of tax benefits, which is good because the less tax you pay, the more money you can keep; and the more money you can keep, the easier and faster you will become wealthy.

Let's briefly go over those tax benefits.

1: Deductions

One way to reduce the tax you pay when investing in real estate is through deductions. The idea is to reduce your taxable income by subtracting specific expense categories. The result is that your taxable base ends up being much, much smaller, lessening your overall tax burden.

What are the various deductible expense categories?

As long as they relate to your trade or business of real estate, they include:

- Mortgage interest
- Property taxes
- Insurance on the property
- Management fees
- Repairs and maintenance costs
- Marketing expenses
- Professional fees
- Business equipment
- Meals with prospective clients and business partners
- Education fees
- Membership fees
- Travel expenses as well as parking fees
- Business communication expenses

These deductibles should highlight the importance of maintaining a record of all your business expenditures because they will come in handy in reducing your overall tax burden.

2: Depreciation

Property generally depreciates over time through wear and tear, which offers another loophole for reducing the amount of tax you pay.

Usually, the depreciation amount is determined based on the expected property's life expectancy and deducted from your taxable income, thereby lowering your tax burden.

Additionally, capital expenditures—attempts made to preserve a property's depreciating value—are deductible from the taxable income depending on your capitalization policies. For instance, if you install a new roof, you can deduct the amount from your taxable income over the useful life of your roof.

It's worth mentioning here that depreciation is only available to properties built for investment purposes.

3: Capital gains tax

Another tax benefit available to real estate is the capital gains tax.

When you purchase an asset that increases in price, then sell it, you have profited in the form of capital gains. Thus, you are subject to a different form of taxation scheme called capital gains tax.

The benefit of capital gains tax is that it is lower compared to the all-too-familiar income tax.

The Federal government classifies capital gains into short-term and long-term. Short-term capital gains involve profits earned from buying and holding onto a property for less than a year. The tax levied on this form of income will range from 10 percent to 37 percent.

On the other hand, when you hold onto a property for more than a year (even for one day more), your profit becomes long-term capital gains. The tax the government expects you to pay will range from 0 percent to about 20 percent.

4: Pass-through deduction

This special form of deduction came into effect in 2018 after congress passed the Tax Cuts and Jobs Act.

It allows certain landlords to deduct up to 20 percent of their passive income from real estate and up to 25 percent of employees' salaries. Both can go a long way in substantially reducing the overall tax burden. Additionally, savvy real estate investors often focus their efforts on minimizing their tax liability by taking advantage of certain tax strategies within US tax laws. One such strategy is cost segregation, which is a strategic tax planning tool that has the potential to shelter taxable income by depreciating certain components of a property at an accelerated rate.

These are some of the various tax advantages accorded to you as a real estate investor. I advise you to consult with a professional such as a CPA or tax attorney before you make financial decisions based on these benefits; these deductions have many gray areas that require the insights of a trained professional.

Now, let's keep the ball rolling.

NOTES

Name_____

Address _____

R℞ Chapter Two

Real Estate Economics

Refills_____

M.D _____

"Buy on the fringe and wait. Buy land near a growing city! Buy real estate when other people want to sell. Hold what you buy!"

John Jacob "Jack" Astor IV, real estate business mogul

"Real Estate assets are is not like gold or diamonds ... it's not something you can buy and look at from time to time ... it's a business. You must purchase real estate with a mindset that you are going to run it as a business. You have got to crunch numbers and look at the market ... without any emotion. My first home in Waco, Texas was a nice house that sat on a beautiful lake. I was so enamored by the home that I made the investment without fully understanding the resale market. That was the only real estate investment I ever made where I lost money, and it taught me ... even on a personal home purchase ... to always follow the data."

Dr. Masaki Oishi, Real Estate Investor

In this chapter, we'll cover real estate economics.

When we talk about real estate economics, we're referring to applying good-old economic principles to explain, predict, and take advantage of price directions, supply, and demand patterns in real estate.

Doing this is a good idea because real estate is subject to the same supply and demand forces that influence other investments and the financial markets.

Once you understand the key economic indicators that affect the market, you can participate during the best conditions, reduce your risk, or hedge your positions during bearish market conditions. That is a much sounder investing approach than merely guessing what to do when facing a challenge. And having an intellectual basis for the decisions you make is what often separates the winners from the losers in any game.

The Four Main Economic Factors That Affect Real Estate

The following economic factors have the most impact on the real estate market.

1: Demographics

Demographics refers to the characteristics of a specific segment of the population.

What is the age, gender, level of income, job description, race, spending patterns, or population growth rate?

These factors are essential because they help determine property prices. They also allow investors to assess the kind of properties likely to be in demand.

Think about it this way. Imagine that the numbers reveal that the population in Los Angeles is primarily made of upper-middle-class men and women in their early-late forties to early fifties, who have young families, and make an average of $200,000 a year.

You would likely conclude that this is a fairly affluent demographic, and investing in properties that suit these people's needs would make some economic sense.

One thing you know is that the upper-middle-class demographic usually gets labeled as lavish spenders. They also have an almost desperate desire to demonstrate their high occupation and social status. Given all that, you might consider setting up luxury condominiums.

What if you determine that a particular population demographic in a certain area primarily consists of the baby-boomer generation? You know, the group that was born between 1945 and 1964.

It is a well-known fact that most of them are not retiring, and because most of their children are grown up, they likely live alone. Many of them consider downsizing at this point.

Knowing this, you will be wise to avoid spacious properties not likely to interest and fit this cohort's needs.

2: Interest rates

Interest rates are the other influential factor that impacts real estate markets.

Interest rates define the cost of borrowing money. The higher the interest rates, the more expensive it is to get a loan. The lower the interest rates, the easier it is to get loans.

When interest rates drop to record lows, it fuels a borrowing spree; suddenly, consumers know that securing a mortgage on the cheap will be possible. The demand for real estate usually increases during such periods, creating real estate bull periods.

Now, you should note that interest rates have the opposite effect on equity investments such as REITs. Investors who buy REITs seek to profit from higher interest rates. As such, when interest rates rise, instead of REITs decreasing because of a lack of consumer demand, they increase because of the lower fixed interest rates on their diversified portfolio.

This fact has significant ramifications for you as a real estate investor. It means you have the opportunity to take advantage of both bull and bear market conditions. It means you can always take shelter under REITs when times get bad and interest rates shoot to the moon.

3: The general state of the economy

The real estate market also tends to mirror the economy's ups and downs.

When the economy is doing poorly, real estate investors typically feel the pinch, and when the economy is good, investors are happy.

We measure the overall economic state using various indicators such as the Gross Domestic Product (GDP), Consumer Price Index (CPI), Inflation, Unemployment, Non-farm payroll, etc.

However, the relationship between real estate and the overall economic state can be somewhat complicated. Certain types of properties are highly-sensitive to dips in the economy.

For instance, when the economy isn't doing so well, luxury apartments and hotel rooms are among the first to bear the effect mainly because when people are hurting for money, they quickly dump non-essentials wants. If you don't believe me, just look to how the hospitality industry has suffered in a Covid environment. Furthermore, the lease on hotel rooms is mostly short-term, making it easier for renters to leave once the term is over.

Residential real estate tends to be somewhat resilient during economic downturns because people still need shelter, even when the economy performs poorly.

Thus, it is vital to consider the nature of your involvement during economic downturns because your risk exposure will not be equal across the board.

4: Government policies

Government policies also affect real estate, and certain government-reinforced policies can increase or decrease real estate demand.

For instance, the Federal Reserve System—the central bank—influences interest rates, and as we have seen over time, interest rates can affect the demand for properties.

Tax credits and deductions can also serve to attract investors or consumers into a particular real estate market.

For instance, in the aftermath of the 2008 housing crisis, the real estate market nationwide, particularly in the residential segment, was overly sluggish. That brought some level of concern, and to try to restore activity in the housing market, the government introduced the first-time homebuyer's tax credit.

Based on the National Association of Realtors' findings, this move alone was powerful enough to attract over 900,000 first-time homebuyers. This upsurge was temporary, but it was good enough to help that whole market recover. Such is the power of government intervention.

In other instances, the government can introduce subsidies that will attract both investors and consumers.

Now let's talk about the various types of assets in commercial real estate.

Types of Commercial Real Estate Assets

If you intend to invest in commercial real estate, knowing the various options at your disposal is essential because these assets all present a wide variety of upsides and downsides. You will want to select those that fit your risk appetite or diversify your portfolio to minimize your risk exposure. Keep in mind that real estate, as is the case in many investment sectors, is subject to market cycles that can affect each industry type in a different way and magnitude.

Here are the main asset classes in commercial real estate (CRE).

1: Retail

The first asset class you should be aware of is retail space, encompassing all the buildings that house everything from grocery stores, malls, restaurants, clothing stores, etc. In other words, retail space is any establishment where the public goes in large numbers to shop for goods, services or eat.

A retail space property can have one major tenant, such as Walmart or BestBuy, or several multi-tenant clients in the same establishment.

Advantages

This commercial property type has the following advantages:

1. It's typical for retail tenants to sign long-term lease contracts, lasting from three to ten years. In some instances, a tenant can obtain a long-term lease lasting between 10 to 25 years. In many instances, realtors call these leases triple net leases (or NNN). With this type of lease, as the investor, you won't shoulder the responsibility of paying property taxes, maintenance fees, or insurance, as that is the tenant's responsibility. Thus, with a triple-net lease, your investment risk is considerably low assuming you have conducted the credit review of your tenant.

2. Another benefit is that clients who obtain long-term leases, especially triple-net leases, are usually very financially stable. Thus, as an investor, you won't worry much about stable returns; your cash flow will remain pretty consistent.

3. Where your property hosts several tenants in different business niches, your investment is relatively safe because the risk of virtually all of them going bankrupt at the same time is remote. Having multiple tenants in different fields is a form of diversification, and is generally a good idea.

4. Higher return rates are the other advantage of owning retail space. Compared to residential real estate, retail properties can have a return rate of anywhere between 9 percent and 12 percent.

Disadvantages

The disadvantages of investing in retail space include:

1. Tenants are not easy to secure, especially those that can obtain triple-net leases on a property. It is typical to find buildings with no tenants that remain that way for a long time. In the meantime, you will have to take care of all associated costs including any property taxes associated with the asset

2. The property's price can drop suddenly because the value of a retail property depends on multiple factors beyond just the location; it can also depend on the terms of the leases that tenants sign. When a lease expires or is about to do so, especially a triple-net lease, the property's value can nosedive because tenants who secure such long-term leases do not come that often. That can raise the risk for the property owner/investor.

3. Retail properties are more vulnerable to economic ups and downs. It's easy for the tenants to file for bankruptcy during recessions, thereby posing more risk to you as an investor.

4. The success of these types of properties heavily depends on the location as well as foot traffic. Securing good deals in properties that fit this profile can be difficult and expensive.

5. Since most retail tenants obtain triple-net leases, investors cannot increase rent throughout the lease period. Thus, you cannot benefit from the market influence of rising real estate rental prices.

6. You will need to work to maintain the property's aesthetic value, which can mean extra expenses. The visual appeal attached to retail properties positively correlates to foot traffic and demand from tenants.

2: Industrial

Industrial properties are next in line. These properties typically house factories, manufacturing establishments, research and development centers, warehouses, etc. As the name suggests, these are properties used for industrial purposes.

Advantages

The advantages of investing in these property types are:

1. The first benefit is that you could get a higher return with this type of property. Typically, you can expect an annual rate of 10 percent with this type of property.

2. Next, you have the benefit of stability. The tenants who rent industrial properties tend to be stable and typically agree to longer-term leases lasting three to ten years, sometimes longer (especially if they have heavy equipment), meaning you can rest assured of a steady cash flow for several years

3. Many industrial tenants, especially ones with a retail storefront, assume the costs of maintaining the property, paying taxes and insurance. That lowers your cost of operating this investment to the bare minimum.

4. Fewer emergencies because these businesses only operate during certain hours. The chances of getting called upon during odd hours to fix issues are almost nonexistent, reducing your challenges.

5. There is considerable demand for this type of property, especially in today's e-commerce era. Many online businesses need fulfillment centers, which has raised the need for warehouses, a form of industrial property.

6. The price is usually objective, and when negotiating a sale or a purchase, you can usually expect a fair price. Residential properties typically have subjective pricing due to the owner's or its tenants' emotional attachment. That is unlikely to happen with industrial properties.

Disadvantages

Industrial properties have the following disadvantages:

1. First, finding tenants or their replacements can be especially difficult. Sometimes it takes months— sometimes even a year—to find a tenant who fits the ideal profile. Meanwhile, you will be incurring costs that, given enough time, could put you in financial distress.

2. Second, some properties get built to specifications that meet the first tenant's needs, making it a lot harder to find a different tenant who needs the exact specifications. You might even have to incur extra tenant improvement costs to adjust the property, making it more attractive to other tenants.

3. Industrial properties do not get much recognition from the press, which often provides free publicity for other property types. They are less fashionable, and therefore, less interesting.

3: Office

Office properties are buildings designed for tenants who primarily operate professional practices. They can range from single-tenant properties to multi-tenant complexes, to skyscrapers, and so on.

It is typical for prospective tenants looking for office space properties to obtain long-term leases.

Advantages

Some standout advantages of investing in office space properties are:

1. The long-term nature of the leases signed by tenants of office space properties virtually guarantees the investor a long-term and stable cash flow.

2. An office space property leased to multiple tenants lowers the risk of a single tenant bankruptcy and financial ruination due to unfavorable economic times.

Disadvantages

Office space properties have the following downsides:

1. It is not possible to adjust rents to keep pace with economic conditions, especially during rising markets. The long-term leases give the tenants the advantage of locking in a specific rent for the whole lease term, meaning that you could have a "loss to lease" economic impact, thereby missing out on potentially higher gains (when compared to market) as an investor.

2. It's expensive to finance these properties, since banks sometimes perceive funding these purchases as high risk.

3. You also have to plan parking space, which can present challenges in areas with space limitations.

4. The tenant's financial stability heavily depends on the overall health of the economy. During bad times, you can be relatively sure that most of them will have a hard time making rental payments, which can be risky for you as an investor.

4: Multifamily

The multifamily property class refers to properties designed to hold multiple-family residences. Technically speaking, if a building has more than four residential units (a four-plex), it's considered multifamily and categorized as commercial real estate.

Multifamily properties are among the most popular commercial real estate properties. In the U.S alone, they make up a quarter of all commercial real estate holdings, and for a good reason: shelter is a basic human need!

While people can forgo most other expenditure classes, shelter is a primary consideration. Thus, there will always be a demand for multifamily residential properties, and they are among the safest commercial real estate investments to hold, especially in a troubled market, because of the low volatility.

<u>Advantages</u>

Investing in multifamily real estate properties has the following standout benefits:

1. The most apparent advantage of multifamily properties is they are a less volatile investment. The predictability of returns is relatively certain even during bearish economic times. When a tenant vacates, finding a replacement in a matter of weeks, if not days, is usually relatively easy. After all, it's easier to get a body in a bed than it is to get a business to rent an office or retail space. Moreover, empirical data shows that over the decades, the rental income from multifamily properties deviates very little from the median, meaning you can always be confident about your cash flow. You don't have to bring rents down to earth to attract tenants in a down market. When you think about it, this stability is because practically everyone, especially those with families, need a primary residence. In down markets, homeowners usually become disenchanted with the burdens of owning a home and opt to rent instead because it seems easier. That becomes a favorite choice for investors seeking safety and stability in their investment portfolios.

2. The rent generated by multifamily properties is easy to adjust upwards. Typically, multifamily properties have short-term leases (6 to 12 months), and when the lease expires, you as the landlord can adjust the rents to fit the current market conditions. This fluid rent nature makes

these properties a safe bet against inflation, while also allowing you to profit from a bull rental market.

3. It's easy to get financing for these types of properties. Banks are enthusiastic about jumping into deals that involve multifamily properties and at favorable rates because they are all too familiar with their stable cash flows. That presents a situation of low risk and a stable loan portfolio for them.

4. It's an attractive investment if you wish to own a rental asset that produces passive income. Due to the predictable cash flow, sometimes all you need to do is acquire such a property, turn it over to a competent property management company, and go back to doing whatever else you want to pursue. Thus, there is a low entry barrier, and to invest in multifamily properties, you do not have to be a real estate expert.

5. There is also the advantage of scalability. You don't have to go all-in; you can start with a smaller property and add units with time. It is not unusual to find properties with extensions that present the investor with the option to add more units with time. That's not the case with commercial real estate properties like office and retail, for instance.

6. There is also the benefit of tax advantages. Most of the tax benefits we discussed previously tend to apply the most to multifamily properties.

Disadvantages

The drawbacks of owning multifamily properties include:

1. The first downside associated with multifamily properties is the level of required management intensity. Even though you can outsource this type of work, you will end up paying a bit for it. The involved management tasks include responding to tenant problems, handling payments made through various means, terminating and renewing

multiple leases, etc. All of this can be time and energy taxing, which is perhaps why management companies may charge roughly 3 percent to 5 percent of your rental income for taking on this kind of responsibility.

2. The predictable returns attached to multifamily properties means many well-funded and competitive market players will have an eye for this opportunity as well. Thus, it is a lot more challenging to deal with this kind of well-capitalized competition because you can easily find yourself in a bidding war with much more formidable forces. That can present a situation where you have to partner with a more experienced investor to ensure you have a bit more muscle in the game.

3. Finally, if you opt to buy instead of building from scratch, you'll realize that these properties can be very costly. Typically, multifamily properties are huge, having many residential units. If the property's location is a high-cost metropolitan area, you could easily be looking at a price-point of more than $1 million. And since most banks require you to put up at least 20 percent, you can easily be looking at the cost of $200,000 or more. It is not easy for the average person to come into this kind of money. Even high-income earners often struggle to secure this kind of cash.

As discussed earlier, economic risk factors can and do influence the profitability of your real estate investments. For example, the most recent 2020 pandemic had an impact on each of these real estate sectors. So, what were the effects of the pandemic?

To understand the impact of the pandemic, as well as what the crystal ball for 2021 may predict, MarketSpace Capital dug into the industry and analyzed a number of factors and trends. These included topics such as capital markets, the economy, construction costs, development trends, effects of COVID, regulatory matters, and much more.

Here is what we determined regarding the ...

Unintended Consequences and Societal Impacts Due to COVID

As we have all learned this year, life can be very unpredictable. In fact, normal life in 2020 has been flipped on its head and has tested everyone. So, from a macro-economic level, the following are the observations for various sectors in the real estate industry.

Office space

One of the effects of the Coronavirus has been the movement out of office space, ostensibly for social distancing purposes. It is uncertain as to if this will be a short-term or more permanent impact on office buildings. As we all know, technology has advanced to enable everyone to be connected, whether they are sitting at their desk in an office or sitting at their kitchen table. As such, many folks are seeing the benefits and efficiency of zero commute time, a more efficient workforce, lower facility cost, etc.

Many major companies have already started to permanently get rid of their office space and move to remote working arrangements. British Petroleum, for example, is in the process of permanently shifting almost 50,000 employees towards remote working and flexible workplace layouts over the next 24 months. So, it seems like office space is getting ready for a shock as existing tenant leases come up for renewal over the next 12 to 24 months.

Retail

The International Council of Shopping Centers (ICSC) has historically cautioned retailers that digital technology will influence the brick-and-mortar sales, but, what the ICSC did not see coming, was the large number of tenant defaults, bankruptcies, and downsizings that were as a result of the government-mandated closure of many retailers. What this means is that many 2nd or 3rd tier retailers (higher credit risks) that once never thought a certain shopping center or prime location was in their price range, now can negotiate from a position of strength with desperate landlords that are looking to fill vacated space.

Hospitality & entertainment

Travel and entertainment budgets have been curtailed due to cost cutting directives from top executives, fear and ability to eliminate travel due to zoom and other technology tools which have now become the "new normal." Additionally, many directives, recommendations, and even mandates from federal, state and local authorities are dictating (or strongly recommending) no travel and entertainment

Just like the airline and cruise industries, the hospitality and entertainment industries have been dramatically hit as evidenced by occupancy levels at historically low levels, Average Daily Rates were slashed, 2020 Rev Pars are 48 percent of what they were in 2019, and even though the operators are doing their best to cut variable costs, their fixed costs of debt service, insurance and property taxes remain unchanged. In short, while their revenues have been cut by over 50 percent, their largest fixed costs remain the same.

Industrial, storage, & fulfillment space

Due to increased demand for online purchasing and growing constraints on supply chain, office flex and industrial space demand is growing. As a result of the "at-home shopping, ordering and direct delivery," there will be increased demand for assets such as fulfillment centers, cold storage, and dry storage for online ordering. Furthermore, there seems to be upward demand for additional factories as popularity of onshoring sweeps the nation.

Multifamily

Current economic forces have had an impact on the incomes, livelihood, and savings of many citizens. Many people remain out of work and what may have been a dream to purchase their own home a short 12 months ago, many have chosen to remain in a rental category. Many multifamily assets focus on a "middle class

America" tenant profile, and that sector continues to see strong lease-up, stable rental rates and an ever-increasing occupancy level for this asset class.

Months on end of being stuck in the house or apartment has led people to question their current living conditions. Along with the shift away from offices, private designated workspaces in homes or apartments will be more important. People will be spending more time at home, and as a result spending more time inside the home. For these reasons, people are now looking for larger residential units with private office space and as much yard or common area green space as they can get. Tied to this, and another underlying impact of Covid-19, is that people have also learned to appreciate public outdoor spaces a lot more. Parks, green space, community gathering spaces, even with social distancing, and other outdoor areas have become a very important commodity.

Let's discuss some of the things you can do to mitigate these risks.

Mitigating Risk During a Down Cycle

Now that we know how economic factors can affect the market, how should we reduce the risk of ruin during disfavoring economic times?

Currently, the economy has plummeted as a result of the COVID-19 pandemic, a natural disaster. Besides the health risk, this pandemic has threatened our basic way of life, and for many people their pockets and bank account are close to being empty.

In early 2020, unemployment hit 14.7 percent, a record high not seen since 1948, and while the situation is recovering, things remain unstable.

Stores like Neiman Marcus, J. Crew, and Tuesday Morning have filed for bankruptcy. Malls are like ghost towns, and Tom LaMalfa, president of Cleveland-based TSL Consulting, has predicted that home prices will decline by 20 percent to 30 percent.

The stock market has also seen huge drops. BBC once reported a drop of 29 percent in the Dow, a 33 percent drop in FTSE, and a 27 percent drop in the Nikkei. As you can see so evidently, many people are currently hurting.

The current economic environment notwithstanding, as an investor—in real estate or otherwise—avoiding bankruptcy should be one of your top priorities. Even when things do not look good, you must always have a documented plan of action that helps you remain afloat when things go wrong.

Thankfully, real estate experts have faced many recessions in the past and learned from them. Handling these bad times will certainly not be easy, but it is possible that you might even get some great deals during times such as these.

Here are the measures I use to hedge against these risks. Perhaps implementing one or two of these strategies will also help you mitigate the risk posed to your real estate portfolio (disclaimer: see your account, financial advisor, banker, etc., before using these strategies):

#1: Adopt a long-term mindset

The first thing you should do is adopt a long-term investing view.

Many people go into real estate, or any other investment, with a short-term mindset, wanting to get rich quickly as their primary objective. That is a bad idea.

Do you know why?

First, you have to realize that accumulating wealth is a long-term commitment. Becoming wealthy, and remaining so, usually takes many years of constructive planning, discipline, sacrifice, budgeting, and wise investing.

After surveying millionaires throughout his research work, Dr. Thomas J. Stanley found that the typical American millionaire never crossed the $1 million net worth threshold until they were in their late forties or early fifties.

There is no shortcut to wealth, and most people who attempt to find such paths will fail miserably.

Second, unless you are a full-time professional who can monitor and time the markets like the pros, the nature of your involvement in these markets is purely passive. Real estate speculation works best for active participants; the level of expertise and amount of work required makes it a better fit for anyone who's practicing active involvement.

I have said it before, and I will say it again: *The people who make the most money in real estate (or even the stock market) are the professionals.*

That's because that's their job and they do it every single day. Subtract their cost of living and business expenses from those high returns, and most of them aren't making much more money than you are.

You undoubtedly make the most money in your medical practice, because you've invested a lot of time, money, and effort into it—and continue to do so.

As you probably already know, practically all investments have ups and downs. Bad times in real estate are no exception. If you accept that you have invested for the long haul, you will wait out these periods, knowing the good times will always follow the bad.

That is not a mere guess. Empirical studies have shown that over time real estate values tend to rise.

The recessions, and even the "bubble bursts," will undoubtedly test your resolve, but they are nothing more than minor drawdowns in your overall equity curve. As long as you have a well-diversified portfolio, and you have not exposed yourself to too much unnecessary risk, a little patience will serve you well in the long run.

#2: Go for properties with existing cash flows

Another way to reduce the risk that you will be participating in a purely speculative endeavor is to invest in properties with existing and stable cash flows, which is a lot like investing in dividend stocks.

If you are an avid follower of famed investor Warren Buffet, you will affirm that he is opposed to speculation. That's one reason why all the stocks he invests in pay dividends from the onset. He wants to make money from his investments from the moment he gets involved. That should be your attitude too.

If you find properties that get you started on the right foot, you will have little reason for regret right from the very beginning.

Think about it. If a property is doing well and posting positive cash flows, even during the current tough times, what are the odds that it will survive this period and do even better when the economy turns around? You bet the odds are pretty good. These are the kind of properties you want to get involved with and make part of your real estate portfolio.

#3: Avoid properties with high rent rates

The other thing you can do to lower your risk is to avoid properties in the luxury space—you know, properties that have sky-high and above-the-norm rental rates!

Can you remember why? We touched on it briefly earlier.

These properties will only be good investments to hold during good times when the economy is doing well, and people are "freer" with their wallets and expenditures. In such times, these properties will pay handsome returns. However, once the tough times come calling—and they always do—these same properties will turn into money pits. It doesn't take a savvy genius to figure out this common-sense investing logic.

When trying economic periods come knocking, people are quick to reduce their living costs. To ensure their sanity and survival, they prioritize and eliminate costly non-essentials.

When it becomes clear that their fancy condo or apartment is costing them more money than it should, they will quickly exit and downsize. That makes the luxury property segment a cluster of losers during bad times. If you're not savvy enough to adapt to elaborate strategies that smart experts might use to minimize their exposure or even profit from the situation, you could easily lose money.

Here's the best, simplest solution for this: Invest in properties that charge at par or below the median rent rates in your local market. Investing in such properties is a lot smarter and safer for you in the long run.

#4: Avoid overleveraging and too much debt

Leverage is a double-edged sword.

On the one hand, it can be a useful tool during good times. Using leverage well during bull periods can result in tripling or even quadrupling your returns with minimal investment.

On the other hand, high leverage can be downright injurious to your overall portfolio, if things happen to go against you.

Since you can never predict when things can go wrong in any particular market, I highly advise against overleveraging your investments.

Overleveraging reflects an investing vice that has been the downfall of many naïve investors: wealth greed. Many people become overly optimistic during good times and think they know the market very well, especially how the market will perform in the future.

In short, these investors think they are bulletproof. They throw caution to the wind and disregard the risk involved. Of course, the banks will still do business with these people; their logic is that should the investor default or go bust, they will foreclose and will own most of the property anyway.

As with any business, banks are like vicious sharks that will take advantage of anyone who appears to know little to nothing about what they are doing.

It doesn't take much of a downturn to wipe out an overleveraged investor, leaving the person in a financial hole. Even minor corrections in the market will put these people in an ugly and precarious position.

You want to avoid this at all times!

The key is to keep your leverage at an acceptable level. A good rule of thumb is to keep your leverage at 70 to 75 percent. You want to put up at least 25 percent down whenever you purchase a property. You also want to make sure that you have a debt-coverage ratio of at least 1.15. This means that you always have a 15 percent cushion of operating cash flow to cover the principal and interest payments on your debt. That way, the risk that you will end up owing more on the mortgage than the property's worth is relatively minimal, as will be the chances of the banks foreclosing your properties, putting you right out of business.

#5: *Avoid value-add properties unless they are part of your core investment strategy*

Real estate investing has a strategy that involves taking properties in need of renovation, making the necessary improvements, then either selling them at a premium price, or increasing the rents. This will reduce your expenses and expand the net income. This strategy appeals to many investors; these properties often come steeply discounted, which allows for a higher profit potential or margin.

However, unless you are an experienced, expert-level real estate investor, dealing with such properties, particularly during these challenging economic times, can be the equivalent of flirting with disaster.

Here's why:

First, it's not easy to differentiate good deals from bad ones, given the market is not doing well amidst the current COVID-19 pandemic. Thus, it is easier to get a property at a price equivalent to what you might get from a property in good condition.

Second, there is a good chance that you might underestimate the cost of renovations. Unless you are a skilled negotiator, you probably won't find the cheapest suppliers possible, as you do not have the bulk purchasing capabilities. That is a risky business approach, and the variables that could go against you are far too many.

Unless you have a well-documented plan for handling things in the best and most cost-effective way possible—as we do at MarketSpace Capital—there is no reason to get involved with such properties at this time.

#6: Diversify your holdings

We've talked about diversification at various times now, because its importance is not something we can ever overstress.

The basic idea behind diversification is to realize that any investment could go against you, which is why you should spread your risk across as many unrelated assets as possible.

The basic assumption behind this idea is that if two assets do not correlate, favorable price movements in one asset will counterbalance adverse price movements in another.

Thus, a portfolio deliberately made up of a wide variety of uncorrelated assets will be subject to little risk should a massive downward movement, which almost borders on bankruptcy.

You can diversify your portfolio in any number of ways.

First, you can diversify by investing in a wide range of real estate properties. For instance, you could put a portion of your investment capital in multifamily housing, a portion in retail, a portion in industrial properties, a portion in office properties, a portion in hospitality, and so on. You could even invest in other geographic regions that do not seem to operate on the same level as your local market.

Second, you could invest in a fund or trust that has built a highly diversified portfolio. At MarketSpace Capital, before you trust us with your money and buy-in, we take you through our entire diversified portfolio so that you can ensure your investments don't leave you overly exposed to risks in one asset class.

Third, you could invest a portion of your capital in real estate as a whole.

I previously recommended 20 percent. You could invest the rest in stocks, bonds, commodities, precious metals, options, and so on. This way, you'll almost-guarantee your protection against losing everything, even though 100 percent protection is a fallacy.

#7: Stay on top of macro location data

You always want to put down a bet on a market where there is a continually rising population. If people are moving into a city, especially from other cities, that's a good sign. It's a signal that investing in such a market is as wise a move as any because a population increase often correlates with increased demand for housing.

That is especially true if the data indicates the migration is due to better job opportunities in the area you're considering as an investment choice. You can determine that by looking at changes in household income.

A good rule we stick with here at MarketSpace Capital is that there must be a 3 percent increase in median household income for every 2 percent rise in population. Once we determine this to be the case, we consider this as the first green light benchmark.

It goes without saying that we still look at other compelling factors that might affect our decision, but this is usually a required minimum.

Given all that has taken place in 2020, what do we feel that these macro-economic cycles will dictate for 2021. In short ... should we be leaning into these headwinds in 2021, or should we retreat to the sidelines?

2020 has been an unforgettable year. Yes, all of us have other adjectives we can use to describe their personal 2020 experience, but for purposes of this book I will use the word "unforgettable!"

The economy that started the year at record-setting levels, then saw some of the most violent shifts in unemployment, swings in revenues at both a corporate and personal level, and personal wealth. 401ks that were tied to the US Stock market saw record highs, a rapid decline, then one of the most dramatic recoveries ever witnessed in our lifetime.

There was also the 2020 election cycle from hell that many would like to simply forget. An election that was filled with some of the most polarizing platforms, debates, and campaign strategies, which caused some interesting political debates at the office, around families, and the never-ending news cycles of cable TV.

Everyone has now cast their vote. All the votes have been counted. Election lawsuits are soon to be over. And just like that, the 2020 Presidential election is finally over. With it, the unforgettable year of 2020 will be in the history books.

But what does a Biden/Harris Administration mean for the future of real estate development, construction, investing, and ownership in the United States? What does the roll out of a COVID-19 vaccine mean for our health, consumer confidence, and ability to get back to the life that we once knew?

No matter how divided a society may be, a balance of power in government generally indicates that future policy will remain in line with current policies, despite overtures of change. Furthermore, population counts continue to grow. The last time we checked, no one has made more land! So well-placed real estate, like gold, is in finite supply and always a great long-term investment.

We are at a point that a savvy investor could capitalize on all markets, especially when focusing on foreclosures with solid property fundamentals (hotel, office, retail—all opportunities with quality product). Therefore, real estate is always a good play despite the stock market, President, or parliament. We will feel pain in the short term due to the pandemic that will translate through to commercial real estate, but long-term fundamentals for core locations are sound. As an investor, this is the time to pounce. As a property owner, this is the time to hold. As a property owner on the edge, this is the time to refinance and benefit from some of the historical low cost of capital.

Okay, we have covered a lot and enough about 2020!

You now know the four main economic factors that affect real estate investing, the different types of commercial real estate properties you can invest in, and how to mitigate risk during a downturn period.

Now let's dive deep into the various real estate markets.

NOTES

R CHAPTER THREE

UNDERSTANDING THE DIFFERENT REAL ESTATE MARKETS

"I have always liked real estate: farmland, pastureland, timberland, and city property. I have had experience with all of them. I guess I just naturally like 'the good Earth,' the foundation of all our wealth."

Jesse Jones, entrepreneur, American politician

"The biggest mistake I ever made in investing was opening an account with the Japanese Post Office. In Japan, the Post Office operated a bank as part of the Commercial Banking System. As a young man, I felt dedicated, even encouraged, to support the government and invest and buy the equivalent of a certificate of deposit. I earned less than 2 percent on what I thought was a good, patriotic investment. Yet, when I wanted to get my cash out before maturity, the penalties were severe and the opportunity cost of having 'liquid cash,' was very high."

Dr. Masaki Oishi, Real Estate Investor

It is no secret that real estate as an industry is a very diverse sector with several markets in which to invest.

This chapter shall introduce you to three different, key real estate markets:

1. The primary
2. The secondary
3. Tertiary markets

We will also discuss how the location factor can affect property values and how you can use it to make wiser investment decisions. A lack of understanding in this area is why many investors lose money in real estate.

Additionally, we shall discuss the proprietary 5-step model we use at MarketSpace Capital to select a quality real estate investment.

We've been using this model for years to sort through the vast array of opportunities presented to us and build our core investment portfolio. This chapter will give you a chance to gain insights into our property selection process and benefit directly from our collective experience.

Types of Real Estate Markets

We can use different ways to classify real estate markets. One of the best ways relates to the level of development. We all know that different areas do not develop equally; some have better developmental growth, while others lag.

On this basis alone, we can come up with three types of real estate markets.

1: Primary markets

The first type of real estate market that deserves your attention is the primary or tier 1 market.

This market represents a class of real estate markets that have the most development. All sorts of facilities, amenities, businesses, and services are sufficiently present in tier 1 markets.

An important distinguishing characteristic of this market is a large population; usually, the expectation is that a typical tier 1 market will have a population base of more than 5 million people within the SMSA (Standard Metropolitan Statistical Area).

Think of all the top cities in the U.S: New York, Los Angeles, Boston, Chicago, Washington, D.C, San Francisco, and the likes are all primary real estate markets.

One feature common to these primary markets is that property values and rents tend to be the most expensive. Let's take the example of New York.

Estimates show that the median cost of renting an apartment in New York is $3,475 per month. Keep in mind that this is not a large apartment, only 700 square feet of space, which is typical for most New York apartments.

Now, compare that with a less glamorous city such as Houston, Texas. The average rental cost of an apartment is roughly $1,118, approximately one third of New York rental prices. The interesting part is that the Houston prices represent a much bigger living space than what anyone would get in New York—estimated to be at 880 square feet.

That brings us to another point regarding primary real estate markets: *the most aggressive and heavily-capitalized operators highly dominate them!*

Investors such as Real Estate Investment Trusts (REITs), Private Equity firms, Hedge funds, and others are among the dominant players in these kinds of markets. In fact, many of these investment vehicles have a mandate that they ONLY invest in tier 1 markets. That presents a situation marked by high competition, something often reflected in the high prices bid for these properties.

For this reason, it is difficult, even unwise, for smaller investors to consider operating in these kinds of markets; they are prohibitively expensive, and the returns are not attractive enough to warrant such a massive allocation of limited capital.

Why are these markets so competitive and only favored by the wealthiest of operators? The perceived risk in primary markets is minimal; investing in these markets falls just short of absolutely guaranteeing returns.

No one loves guaranteed investments more than the top firms, because they represent a large class of unsophisticated public investors who demand consistent performance.

Thus, you will find that during economic downturns in real estate, most of the money invested in real estate will be in primary markets because, in such times, people are much more averse to risk, making guaranteed returns a priority.

However, there's one caveat: *The high prices in primary markets are likely to be more inflated than objective evaluations because of the large number of potential buyers, and hence the bidding price wars.* Because of this, these markets are much more prone to bubble inflations and subsequent bursts.

Think about it, what do you think will happen when the top guys keep bidding, driving the price up to the point of it being so ridiculous that no one ordinary person can afford it?

Here's the answer: *The price will suddenly fall off a cliff and always settle to a much more reasonable equilibrium.*

During such times, if you are a small operator, your portfolio could take a huge hit, making this yet another reason why you should avoid this type of market, despite its inherent attractiveness. Unless you're okay with the idea of getting burned, you should leave these markets to the big investment firms and trusts, a.k.a., the big boys.

Another reason not to get involved in tier 1 markets is that the potential return on a property investment relative to its inflated cost—also called the cap rate—is not very attractive; it tends to be amongst the lowest in this market. For instance, a recent estimate from TruePoint Capital found the median cap rate to range from 2 percent to 4 percent in tier 1 markets.

Comparatively, other markets that do not qualify as primary markets have higher cap rates that range from 5 percent to 7 percent. In short, for each dollar paid for the asset, it is generating five to seven cents in net operating income.

2: Secondary markets

After primary markets, you have secondary markets, also called tier 2 markets.

The infrastructural development in secondary markets is quite developed and ongoing. However, by many estimates, the developmental growth in secondary markets falls a little behind primary markets.

The best way to think of secondary markets is "up and coming," the same way we define an actor, musician or Double-A baseball player, who shows great promise of making it to the big leagues as "up and coming artists or player." It is pretty much the same thing when it comes to secondary markets: these markets show great potential and have a lot to be proud of, but they are not there yet.

One noteworthy thing about secondary markets is the *population*. Secondary markets have a population range of as low as one million people to as many as five million in the SMSA.

At this point, you can probably guess which cities would qualify as secondary markets. Think of cities like Seattle, Pittsburgh, Baltimore, Austin, Detroit, Atlanta, Salt Lake City, Charlotte, Denver, Miami, Seattle, and others.

These are your typical, well-known cities that don't boast of super-high status just yet. They're almost hot but are not there just yet. However, given enough time and investor activity, they will eventually morph into primary markets.

Secondary markets are suitable investment opportunities for many reasons. One such reason is that they offer great promise for high returns and do not pose significant risks due to tough competition.

For instance, properties in a secondary market are considerably less expensive compared to those in the primary market. In the last example, we looked at the median rent for an apartment in Houston, Texas. We saw how prices might be three times—perhaps more—cheaper than those in primary markets. That example might shed some light on why investors favor secondary markets, especially during booming economic periods.

When times are good, as an investor, you can expect to find favorable property deals in the secondary market, and many of which are likely to turn a good profit. During these times, the perceived risk in these markets is minimal, and people are enthusiastic about jumping at the chance for higher returns.

However, the opposite tends to happen when things get tough. Remember, facilities and amenities in secondary markets are still underdeveloped, or developing. As such, those in the primary market become more desirable.

During recessions, investors become more hesitant to invest their dollars in these markets because they perceive them as riskier. Many of those with deep pockets will take off and concentrate their efforts in the more developed cities that form the primary market.

At MarketSpace Capital, we believe in the potential found in secondary markets. We do not believe in the cut-throat competitive spirit, and the distasteful returns lurking in the primary markets. That's why a vast portion of our portfolio has properties in the secondary markets class. We're confident in our programmatic approach to selecting quality properties we deem to be good investments.

Later in this book, we will reveal and show you how to implement the real estate investing approach that has helped us grow our asset under management portfolio to over $250 million.

For now, let me mention this: We focus on secondary markets for one reason. We are aware that bad times in primary markets will often benefit secondary markets.

For instance, when rent prices rise to astronomical levels, and out of the blue a sudden downturn happens in the economy, you can bet that most of the primary market tenants will be looking to downsize. That often means moving from affluent metropolitan neighborhoods located in the major cities to the less descript, but habitable, residences.

Moreover, many businesses find the low operating costs afforded by secondary markets attractive, and during economic downturns, they are eager to move their operations into these areas quickly.

Since most businesses have the flexibility to pick up their team and move to more efficient locations, their movement into secondary markets often sparks an influx of job seekers into these cities, leading to a population increase.

In essence, if you're hopeful about investing in the future, secondary markets are the best place to consider. Primary markets don't offer much room for improvement because, as I mentioned earlier, primary markets are the primary playground for the big financial institutions that have little or no entrepreneurial flair in them and the pricing has many inflated characteristics. Most are primarily interested in moving around assets and playing it safe, all while charging hefty transaction fees instead of generating actual profits.

3: Tertiary markets

Lastly, we have *tertiary markets*, also called tier 3 markets. Tertiary markets represent the least developed real estate markets.

The infrastructure here is massively underdeveloped and will likely not improve significantly in the short-term. It may also interest you to know that these markets have low populations. It is typical for them to have populations under 1 million. Given these facts, you might even think of these markets as being asleep.

However, in terms of growth potential, these markets offer the greatest opportunity. Investment experts have observed that the employment and population growth numbers in these markets rival those in the primary and secondary markets. Also, since properties in tertiary markets haven't developed much, you can bet on the availability of plenty of land assemblages to support new property developments.

Perhaps the most standout benefit associated with tertiary markets is the relative ease of acquiring properties and finding deals. Tertiary market properties are cheap, affordable, and easy to find. As such, the pricing is reflective in the Cap Rates. Thus, you do not have to worry much about burgeoning costs when finding and striking deals.

The main problem associated with tertiary markets is that their underdeveloped infrastructure presents a risk for investors. It is difficult for investors to smell quick returns in these markets because once you make your investment, you have a smaller universe of buyers in which to sell and exit your investment.

The only time when these markets become attractive is during booming economic periods. During such times, investors will be happy to participate because most will be envisioning above-average returns from these kinds of markets in the long-term.

However, when times are bad, investors have a low appetite for the risk of investing in tertiary markets, especially when compared with the previous two markets.

Throughout our discussion about the different real estate markets, you may have realized something: location is everything. This is why realtors use this trendy phrase:

Location, Location, Location

For good reason, location is a good real estate aphorism; it's one of the most standout factors influencing a property's value. No matter how good a property's condition, amenity package and economics, it won't fetch good returns if the location is inconvenient.

Now, you might be asking yourself, "How do I go about evaluating the location characteristics of a property?"

That's a good question as the idea of location by itself doesn't mean much to the average person. You need to know which location elements you need to pay attention to; otherwise, "location" is just another meaningless phrase.

Let's go over various objective characteristics that a well-located property might have.

1: Proximity to a CBD

CBD stands for Central Business District. In certain cities, it has another name: the financial district or downtown. Simply put, the CBD is the part of a city where the main business and commercial activities and operations are.

Now, given this, it's clear that the more developed a city is, the less room there will be for more improvement. Thus, land in or near a CBD tends to be a very scarce commodity indeed, and as you already know, scarcity tends to create value.

That brings me to my main point:

The closer a property is to a city's financial district, the higher its value tends to be. And the opposite tends to be true. The farther away a property is from the CBD, the lower its value.

For instance, consider New York City. You can expect properties in areas like Manhattan to go for a lot more than properties in other metropolitan areas like Beacon, East Hanover, Bronxville, etc.

According to Zillow, the median cost of a home in Manhattan is $632,271. Comparatively, the average price of a home in Bronxville is $497,090. Can you see the significant difference, even though both are New York neighborhoods? The difference is that one is closer to the financial district than the other.

I point this out to you because it can affect your decision making. Knowing how the CBD location affects property prices makes it easier to decide which property to choose based on your financial commitments: one near or further away from the CBD.

Sure, we have only looked at residential properties because the data has solely focused on home prices. However, the rule remains accurate for any property, including those in the commercial sector.

Data from the Bureau of Census Data on Urbanized Areas has indicated that when a city experiences outbound migration, the outlying metropolitan areas are the first ones to be vacated. Therefore, they tend to take the worst hit in terms of price.

2: The quality of a neighborhood

We can also assess the location factor in terms of the neighborhood's desirability in which a property (or planned development) exists. This factor is particularly significant if you are considering multifamily housing.

A property in an area replete with gangs and low-income earners will certainly go for less than a property in an area filled with high educational attainment with good incomes and high-security provisions.

You should note that judging a neighborhood's quality can be very subjective. However, three critical factors can add objectivity to your assessment.

The first one is accessibility. How easily accessible is a neighborhood? Is it closer to major transit routes that serve the city? How many alternative routes can access the area?

Remember, going to work will be a part of the average tenant's everyday life. A vast majority of them will work in the city, meaning a neighborhood that tenants will favor, a neighborhood that makes getting to work easier over one that makes the same thing tougher.

With that in mind, a neighborhood located closer to major transit routes with many entry points will be more desirable than one located farther away, with only a few access roads serving it.

Next, you have to consider the appearance of the neighborhood itself. Is it appealing? First, what is the general condition of properties in the area? Are they well kept, or are they in need of a significant makeover?

How good—or bad—is the landscaping? Can you spot manicured lawns and trimmed hedges? Do the residents care about their surroundings? Can you see nearby parks and community spots? What about trees? Can you spot a number of them?

By the way, trees add to the aesthetic value of a neighborhood. If you can spot a number of them, preferably more, and in an area bordering the city, the better.

You also want to consider the presence of amenities. Do you have shops, grocery stores, restaurants, and such nearby? Many people like to have the presence of such facilities within easy reach. If someone has to travel miles to access such facilities, the less desirable the neighborhood is generally.

Let's not forget about schools; the quality of nearby schools is vital to a neighborhood's overall quality.

Many tenants—and even buyers—who can pay top dollar for property want the best education possible for their children. If the nearby schools boast good grades and facilities, more points go for the neighborhood as a whole.

Security is another vital factor. What is the state of security in the area? What is the overall crime rate? More importantly, do the residents feel safe in the community? Do you have private security firms offering services in the area? Is there a presence of law enforcement premises within reasonable reach, i.e., what is the average response time?

Lastly, you will want to gauge how fast properties stay on the market. Typically, real estate agents will have access to this kind of information because they get involved in listing properties and closing most deals.

If properties don't stay long on the market before someone else jumps in to grasp the opportunity, then you know you are looking at a desirable neighborhood. Obviously, the contrapositive of this statement is also true.

3: Plans for future developments

While present amenities are certainly vital to the property's current value, future developments are likely to influence property value even more. Therefore, you want to make sure you do your homework and identify all planned developments.

Is there a hospital under construction in the area? Is the construction of a new school underway? What about new roads? Are any of them currently under construction or in the planning phase? What is the Capital Improvement Plan (CIP) of the city and county, and where are they allocating their investment dollars?

Another thing you should also consider is the development of new residential and commercial buildings. For instance, is there a new mall under construction or consideration?

These future developments can impact a property you are considering in any number of ways, either positively or negatively.

For instance, imagine you have a property with an incredible view of a city, mountain, forest, or anything along those lines. When a residential property gets constructed close to it, and it happens to block the view that was your main selling point, the price of your property could drop suddenly. However, if you happen to own an office building and find out that there is a planned road construction close to it, you know that this will work in your favor because of the improved accessibility.

4: Proximity to public facilities

A property's proximity to public facilities can also affect its price. For example, consider a multifamily property, a place people reside in and call home. What impact do you suppose a busy highway will have on the property's desirability? How many people will want to live there and deal with the uncontrollable noise of speeding vehicles?

Now consider other facilities such as hospitals, fire stations, schools, churches, or community centers. Their impact will likely be the same.

On the other hand, the impact could be slightly opposite for property types like office buildings and retail. The presence of a nearby highway, commercial property, or a gas station will likely positively affect the value of such properties.

5: The size of the lot

The size of the lot on which a property sits is an influential factor to consider. Usually, it matters less if a building's quality is good and the land beneath it is considerably small. Do you know why?

It's because a house is a depreciating asset. Can you remember the depreciation cost deductions we talked about earlier, the ones that can reduce your taxable base?

Conversely, raw land is an appreciating asset whose value tends to rise over time. Think about the implications of that for a moment.

It means that when presented with the option of choosing between two properties, one with a recent construction that sits on ½ an acre lot, along with another older building that sits on an acre, you may be better off going with the second option. In the long run, the second deal will likely end up being a better investment for you if you manage the costs of renovating it properly.

Based on these five factors, you no longer have to worry about the vagaries of the mantra: location, location, location.

Let's move on and talk about the model we use at MarketSpace Capital to make property investment decisions.

How to Identify the Best Investment Opportunities: An Econometric Model

Earlier, I mentioned that if you are ever going to survive and thrive in real estate, you need a definite and systematic approach that guides your decision-making process.

Having such a model isn't just true in real estate; practically every business could benefit from having a systematic operational approach. Take, for instance, the world of banking. Without a doubt, the banking world is one of the most stable sectors of our economy.

Banking has thrived for centuries. Some of the giants in the business have been in the business for longer than anyone can imagine. For example, Samuel Osgood and the 14 founding directors founded Citibank, one of the largest banking firms, in the world today, in 1812. Henry Wells and William Fargo founded Wells Fargo, another big-name bank, in 1852.

Today, they are still alive and well; they seem to thrive with each passing year. None of us can question the success these banks have achieved. However, when you look under the hood, you'll notice that there're all kinds of risks inherent to the banking business itself.

First, there's usually the risk that a venture might not work. Banks lend money to businesses that may or may not go bankrupt, and in case you didn't already know, business failure rates are pretty high, and banks need to manage the risk in a way that will keep them solvent.

Second, there's usually a lot of money at stake. A bank can fund the construction of a piece of property worth hundreds of millions of dollars. Anything can go wrong, and the bank can lose a fortune in the process. And let's not forget the fact that banks leverage deposits from clients and other sorts of risks I can't talk about in great detail.

Yet, many banks manage to stay afloat and rake in profits each year. How is this possible?

One important reason is that banks operate systematically and have significant oversight, rules and regulations by federal examiners. Perhaps no area of business pays attention to systems more than banks. Banks rely heavily on ratios and all sorts of math-based criteria that guide their decisions. Banks never operate on emotion; it's just too risky, and they can't afford that.

A bank won't lend money to every person. They conduct a considerable amount of due diligence before arriving at a decision. If things check out, the bank will assume the risk with confidence. Bankers figure that by operating this way, they reduce the risk of going out of business while increasing the chances of turning a profit.

You must do the same!

You must have a set of documented guidelines that help you determine when you can and cannot act in any given situation. Having such a set of guidelines will reduce the chances of getting into bad deals that could land you in the poor house.

With that mentioned, and as promised, we shall now talk about the 5-step system we rely on at MarketSpace Capital to make critical decisions regarding the kind of investment risks we wish to take on at any given time.

So far, this system has proven valuable over the years we have been in business—to the tune of $250 million in assets under management— and we deem it to be very sound. It is certainly a far cry from operating in a cavalier, shoot-from-the-hip kind of attitude that has driven many naïve investors into financial troubles.

For disclosure purposes, I must say that there have been times when things didn't go as expected. However, because this five-step system emanates from experience and empirical data, we've always chosen to stick to our system because we believe it has a sound economic basis; many situations have turned around and even shown a profit. In other words, this is the "secret sauce" that has kept us in business both in good and bad times.

Let's jump right in and take a look at it.

Step #1: A city that has a growing population that reflects population migration from other cities

There is no point in placing your money where the general population is declining.

Remember that your money comes from somewhere. Someone has to rent your place for you to make money. Too many investors assume that investing in a property entitles them to returns. Well, that isn't the case.

Yes, you might accidentally put your money in the right market without performing any due diligence, but counting on such luck is a fool's approach because nobody gets lucky every time. Instead, it's a lot smarter to do your research and come up with hard evidence on the merits of investing in a market you are considering.

The problem with investing in a market with generally declining populations is that you could be looking at a scenario of oversupply and insufficient demand. When that happens, you might be in for a situation where you have to compete aggressively for tenants, which might cause you to lower rental rates. You don't want that. Instead, go for a market that virtually guarantees tenants a few weeks after the contractor completes the project. If you are buying, go for a property already filled with tenants.

The best way to identify such a market is by examining population data trends. Is the population generally rising or declining? If it is growing, by how much?

You also want to determine the possible reasons for people's migration into the city you are considering. Preferably, you want people to move into a city for employment reasons. When people move into a city because of increased employment opportunities, you can be confident that you have a good market.

Here's what we look for in population growth data:

- If the population is around 1 million or less, you want to check for a growth rate of at least 1.5 percent or more.

- At a population of 2 million or less, a growth rate of 1 percent or more is ideal—at MarketSpace Capital, we consider this a requirement.

- If you are looking at a small town with a population of 250,000 or less, you should aim for a growth rate of at least 3 percent or more.

In other words, if the size of a population is small, only go for the property if the population data shows a higher growth rate. Conversely, a larger population will only require a minor positive change to justify its selection as a potential investment opportunity.

A classic example would be Detroit.

Many property investors have suggested that this market is in a rebound state. If you buy into this statement, then you would be too excited to jump at such an opportunity. After all, if other people say that this market is hot, then it must be true, right? Wrong! You need to perform your analysis and reach a personal conclusion on whether the facts support the notion.

Besides, no matter how good they are, other people have a unique set of criteria and bias upon which they base their judgments. Their strategy has nothing to do with your decisions. When you base your decision to invest on such opinions, you're likely to end up in a worst-of-both-worlds situation that unlikely will not end well for you.

According to the United States Census Bureau, in 1950, Detroit had a record high population of 1.8 million people. As of 2017, it had a population of merely 673,014 people; that's a sharp population decline over time.

Even a look at more recent population estimates reveals a consistent downtrend. In 2010, the population stood at 711,043. If you compare that figure with the recently reported figure of 673,014, the downtrend will be clear to see. Thus, the idea that the Detroit economy is in a virtual rebound has no basis in reality. The data available contradicts that hypothesis, and any wise investor would stay away from that market.

Step #2: A rise in median household income

You also want to confirm that people have money to spend because if money is tight, most people will be conscientious about allocating their financial resources. When people hold on to their money too much, there won't be much renting going on, which could spell trouble for your investment project.

How do you avoid the income-to-spend problem? Again, you look at the data. When things are good, the median (typical or average) income should go up.

Here, it's best to look for a 3 percent increase in median household income for every 2 percent population increase. Once you have a minimum of such a combination, you have the green light to proceed.

I know what you're thinking, "Mas, how exactly do I get your hands on this kind of data?"

The good news is that we live in the information age, and if you're willing to look for it, there're plenty of data tools to help you with this kind of research, many of which are free. One such tool is City-Data: http://www.city-data.com/

The City-Data website allows you to look up all kinds of demographic data related to a particular city. This data is worth its weight in gold, especially when you're using a model such as the one we're talking about to make core investment decisions.

It's almost unbelievable that all this wealth of information is available to the public at no cost whatsoever. The truth is that you may end up performing all your research without ever leaving this website. There is no reason why you shouldn't use it.

Step #3: Vacancy rate

The vacancy rate is the percentage of units that are not occupied units in a particular rental property; it's the opposite of the occupancy rate, defined as the number of tenant-occupied units.

You determine the vacancy rate by multiplying the number of vacant units by 100 and dividing the result by the total number of units within in a property.

The vacancy rate matters because it is another key indicator of market performance and the ease of earning returns in a particular market. A high vacancy rate points to a problem with demand and vice versa.

Now, it's not easy to establish the vacancy rate in a particular market as a whole. However, you can get a clue.

One quick way to get an idea of whether the vacancy rate is high or low is to assess the speed at which new rental properties are getting off the market. If properties are selling fast, then the vacancy rate must be low. If they are taking longer to sell, then the vacancy rate must be somewhat high.

Think of it this way: Put yourself in the shoes of an investor tasked with the challenge of investing a certain amount of dollars and get returns on them no matter what. If you were this person, would you go for a nearly empty property, or would you go for one filled with tenants and vacancies that are easy to fill in a matter of days?

You know the answer! It's pretty commonsense stuff, which is perhaps why other investors have the same reasoning. It's no wonder, then, that investors competitively bid for properties with a low vacancy rate. Such properties are like money in the bank for them.

You can get an idea of how fast rental properties are getting off the market by consulting local real estate agents. They have considerable first-hand knowledge of the current happenings in the market.

Step #4: The level of crime

You also want to make sure you pay attention to a city's crime levels and trends. As a rule, places with low crime levels are more desirable than areas with constant crime reports.

Why is this the case? There are many reasons, but I will highlight two primary ones.

1. First, people fear for their safety, because of which, they'll always choose to live in areas where they're unlikely to get robbed at gunpoint or harassed by street gangs.

2. Second, areas with high crime levels usually point to low literacy levels. When literacy levels are low, you can expect locals to have low incomes too. Therefore, investors who are seeking high and consistent returns on their investments do not favor such areas.

With that noted, how do you establish if a city is a safe-enough place to invest? At MarketSpace Capital, we believe that a crime index score of 500 or less indicates an area characterized by relative safety. Conversely, any score above the 500 mark makes a neighborhood unsafe and risky.

Let's take a look at a case in point.

Example

Consider the city of Columbus in Ohio. Looking at the crime records assembled by city-data.com, we can establish that in 2003, the crime index score was at 714, which is above our threshold by a significant margin. In such a case, we would advise you to avoid such a market at all costs.

However, over time, things changed for the better. The latest data shows that the score is at 419, a significant improvement, especially considering that the trend has been steadily heading downwards since 2005.

Now, if all other criteria check out, Columbus might be a good market to consider investing in.

Step #5: Annual job growth

It should be evident that if people are struggling to find jobs, then the economy is not in an overall good state. People need money to sustain themselves, and when they don't have it, they certainly won't be doing any business with you or anyone else for that matter.

Therefore, it's essential to assess the job market in any particular area. Before you decide to invest, endeavor to determine whether employers are moving into or out of a specific market.

If a location has an adequate supply of job opportunities, it means there is greater disposable income that people can spend, and therefore it offers a higher migration rate into the area. All these two scenarios work to your advantage.

At MarketSpace Capital, we believe in having at least a 2 percent annual job growth rate in a particular area to conclude that there is enough job safety to warrant our involvement in that specific market. We urge you to do the same.

Also, make a point of studying the unemployment trends. In Columbus, for instance, the data shows that unemployment has been taking a nosedive consistently since 2010, which is a good sign.

That concludes our five-step model for selecting investment opportunities. Now you know enough to make critical investment decisions when considering which property investments to make and which ones to avoid.

We are confident that adhering to this five-step process will make it unlikely to make an investment that will give you poor returns. More importantly, we're sure that if you follow this systematic approach, volatile economic periods will have a hard time knocking you out of the game and that in the long run, you will be a winner.

In the next chapter, we will continue the conversation but go deeper, looking at how you can analyze specific investment opportunities.

R CHAPTER FOUR

EVALUATING REAL ESTATE INVESTMENT OPPORTUNITIES

"Games are won by players who focus on the playing field—not by those whose eyes are on the scoreboard. If you instead focus on the prospective price change of a contemplated purchase, you are speculating. There is nothing improper about that. I know, however, that I am unable to speculate successfully, and I am skeptical of those who claim sustained success at doing so."

Warren Buffett, billionaire investor

"Apart from my first home, which had an abysmal investment return, every single real estate investment I have made has been profitable. I have never faced a situation where we lost money on a deal. Yes, some have taken longer than anticipated to sell the property and some where we had to renegotiate terms of finance. Yet by surrounding myself with a team of professionals, we are able to structure the investment and understand the market, economics and timing of cycles. After all, real estate is a fixed asset, and in the end, it can stay in place until the market cycles come back to equilibrium."

Dr. Masaki Oishi, Real Estate Investor

Let's take a trip further down the rabbit hole and talk about other strategic approaches you can use to evaluate investment opportunities and perform your due diligence to reach various real estate investing decisions.

Defining Value-add, Development, and Stabilized Properties

One way you can look at risk in a real estate deal relates to the amount of work a property requires before you can realize expected gains either in the form of rental income or profits from a sale.

Generally, the more work a property requires, the higher the perceived risk in the situation. That's because it requires time, effort, and money to make all those critical adjustments, and, as you can imagine, a lot could go wrong when taking such corrective steps.

Now, based on this premise alone, we can come up with three ways to classify properties, as follows:

1: Value-add properties

Value-add properties are the first class of properties. Value-add properties are properties believed to be performing below their true market potential due to any number of factors.

With these properties, the steps that an investor has to take to reposition these property types in the market is the primary challenge.

Some issues common to value-add property are:

- Bad management
- Capital repairs
- Low occupancy rate
- Low lease rates
- Less than satisfactory facilities

- Minor design flaws

The basic idea is to improve the property's image to prospective tenants, thereby increasing its revenue potential.

Value-add properties are an excellent fit for investors who have a medium-level risk appetite and looking for above-average returns.

2: Development properties

- These property types are sometimes also called opportunistic or green-field properties. They involve a lot more work than value-add properties, and because of it, many property investors consider them the riskiest form of investment.

- Usually, development properties involve a substantial amount of construction, therefore, not only do you have the traditional market risk, you also have development and lease-up risk.

- Therefore, these kinds of projects favor professionals because they usually involve a myriad of issues. Some of these issues include:

- Obtaining permits and entitlements from relevant government authorities

- Securing labor and required materials cheaply

- Obtaining loans from financial institutions to fund construction work

- Projecting the income level to be generated once construction completes and the building gets leased, or the possible resale value.

As you can imagine, returns from development properties are pretty substantial.

However, given the complicated nature of your involvement with these properties, I would never recommend that passive investors pursue these kinds of projects. Investing in development properties is nothing short of speculation. As I mentioned earlier, speculation is a business that needs active handling, using a hands-on manner, with particular attention paid to detail.

The only exception I can think of is a situation where you can partner up with an experienced professional who will agree to take care of the hard work involved.

At MarketSpace Capital, we can afford to take on these projects because we have a team of specialists at our disposal and the relevant experience. If you're determined to invest in developmental properties, you are better off getting involved with an experienced company and team.

3: Stabilized, core properties

Last, we have core properties.

This property class involves the least amount of work, if any at all, and for this reason, many investors consider it the safest bet.

In many cases, you will find that a stabilized property has a near-100 percent occupancy rate. Also, with these properties, physical or operational improvement is pretty minimal. Moreover, these properties are usually strategically-located in established markets such as tier I and II.

Given this, with these properties, you can expect a positive cash-flow from the moment you get involved. Without a doubt, these properties are the most conservative forms of investment in real estate.

They are perfect for those who have little tolerance for risk and prefer predictable cash-flows. For example, if you are a retiree looking for investment income to take care of you in your remaining years, these properties may be a better fit than their higher risk alternatives.

Differences Between Classes A, B, and C Properties

The variance between classes A, B, and C properties is another way of measuring and classifying the risk involved in real estate properties. This method is more reliable than the previous one because it accounts for multiple factors such as:

- The age of the property
- The income level of tenants
- The location of the property
- Growth potential
- Level of appreciation
- Level and predictability of cash-flows

Based on these factors, we can come up with three property classes.

1: Class A properties

Class A properties are the most attractive class of properties. The properties in this class are generally newer, usually constructed within the last 15 years. The architecture has a modern design, and the quality of materials and amenity packages used during construction is pretty high. They also produce the highest and most predictable cash-flow, mainly because of their location—in established markets—and cater to high-income-generating tenants.

Another crucial characteristic is that these properties have little to no maintenance issues, implying that they are the cheapest to acquire and keep. The management is typically professional grade, meaning you can always count on less involvement in the day-to-day operating details.

Given these facts, Class A properties involve the least amount of risk, and many conservative investors consider them the safest bet. Competition for these properties is pretty high, implying that you will always acquire them at a low cap rate.

NOTE: We will talk more about cap rates later in this chapter.

2: Class B properties

Next are Class B properties. These properties represent a risk level positioned in the middle along the scale. In terms of age, they are a little older than Class A properties and may, therefore, have maintenance issues. Also, the management of these properties may present problems that needs adjustment.

Additionally, these properties are in less affluent locations, and the tenants typically earn lower incomes. Therefore, these properties' rental rates are slightly lower than the conventional, Class A properties.

The attractiveness associated with Class B properties has more to do with the fact that the vast majority of them are value-add type properties. Competition for these kinds of properties is far less than Class A properties.

Therefore, Class B properties offer real estate investors a chance to step in, invest a bit of sweat equity, make improvements, and reposition the property on the market to earn a higher return on investment.

3: Class C properties

Class C property types have the highest associated risk level. This class represents the oldest buildings, usually older than 20 years. Because of their age, repositioning them in the market requires significant repairs and maintenance. The cost of such adjustment is often very high, making them less desirable to conservative investors.

These properties also tend to be in less desirable locations, such as tier III markets, and their tenants are usually low-income earners, making the rental income considerably lower.

If you have a high-risk tolerance, an entrepreneurial outlook, and believe in the potential of these kinds of properties, you are likely to thrive with them. Competition for these properties is far lower, and you can acquire them at great bargains, leaving excellent profit margins.

At MarketSpace Capital, we tend to invest in Class B properties because, over time, we have grown impressed by their potential for above-average profits. We believe that if we perform our due diligence with these properties, the risk associated with our involvement is considerably low.

Now let's talk about property valuation.

Principles of Real Estate Valuation

How do you tell how much a property is worth?

That is a question you will have to answer if you want to buy property, sell it, acquire insurance, or pay property taxes.

Given that you will regularly encounter these situations, you cannot overlook the importance of having a basic idea of what goes into determining a property's value. Generally, you need to be aware of three main ways of property valuation. These are as follows:

1: The market comparison approach

The market comparison model is the simplest and most widely applied of the three; it is also called the *bricks-and-mortar valuation model*. If you are a relative real estate rookie, you can rely on this model to come up with a quick estimate of your property's worth.

Here is how it works.

You look at the price that comparable properties have sold for recently. That price most likely reflects your property's market value. You should note that the comparable properties used to arrive at the value estimate must have similar features such as lot size, number of rooms, square footage, condition, age, etc.

A professional valuation expert will usually be aware of the subtle differences between the comparable properties and account for those differences in the valuation calculations to arrive at a more accurate assessment.

Banks and other major lenders tend to favor this kind of valuation model to estimate a property's worth before financing a purchase.

2: The income/investment approach

Another reasonably popular valuation model is the income/investment approach. This method looks at the current income generated by a property, or the potential income, and uses it as a basis for coming up with a value estimate.

Owners and operators of commercial real estate properties are especially fond of this method. It's working modalities are a bit complicated, but once you figure out the formula, it isn't intimidating.

Here's how it works.

First, you determine the gross income a property generates. You can do this by obtaining all income statements from the property when it has a near-100 percent occupancy rate.

Next, you establish the effective gross income, the figure reflecting the expected gross income by factoring in possible future vacancies, as concisely as possible. The best way to arrive at this figure is by estimating vacancy costs, which you can do by looking at the vacancy rates and costs associated with comparable properties.

Next, you determine the expenses associated with running the property, both fixed and variable, including property taxes, utilities, management fees, payroll, etc.

Once you have all this information, you can determine what we call the Net Operating Income (or NOI), a figure determined by subtracting property expenses from the effective gross income.

Last, you determine the property's value by dividing the Net Operating Income by the Cap Rate. For now, I want you to think of a cap rate simply as a property's estimated return on investment (I have mentioned, we'll delve a bit deeper into Cap Rates).

NOTE: The way you arrive at the appropriate Cap Rate to use for your calculations is by examining those of comparable properties. In essence, the formula boils down to the following:

$$\text{Property Value} = \frac{\text{Net Operating Income}}{\text{Cap Rate}}$$

3: The cost approach

The last model we shall discuss is the cost approach, often favored by owners and operators of properties that are not easy to sell, such as schools and government facilities. Insurers also prefer it.

The basic idea is that a property's value is a direct function of the value of the land upon which it sits, plus the costs of replacing the property, such as after fire damage. This equation also includes the estimated depreciation cost.

The value of land is usually determined by examining comparable properties and coming up with rough estimates. On the other hand, the cost of replacement can be arrived at through several means. The most common one is establishing the actual cost of constructing properties with comparable square footage and multiplying the resulting figure with the primary property's total square footage.

These are the three main ways used in real estate to establish a property's market value. It is important to note that market value doesn't always equal price. In many cases, a property can sell for below market value, such as when an owner is trying to attract bids quickly. In other instances, especially in hot markets, properties can sell above fair market value. Either way, the true definition of fair market value is what a willing buyer and a willing seller transact at the time of sale for a property.

Now you know the formulas used to determine property valuation, let's discuss another element you have to master as a real estate investor: negotiating deals.

The Art of the Deal: How to Negotiate a Real Estate Investment Transaction

If you hire a professional property appraiser, the person will handle all the valuation work we've mentioned above. I recommend using the professional appraiser route with every deal you're considering to ensure you know a property's fair market value. Once you know the fair market value, you can choose to whether or not to enter into a negotiation with a seller.

Negotiation is a tough process, one that very few people know how to navigate. The idea of quibbling over price may even sound abhorrent to you.

For that reason, I recommend entering the negotiation process accompanied by a skilled negotiator. A top real estate agent usually fits this role, and you want to make sure the agent feels properly incentivized to get you a great deal.

You can agree, for instance, that on top of the commission, you will provide a handsome bonus for every $10,000 or $100,000 the agent can have the price reduced. This approach is a lot better than negotiating personally, especially if you're "just winging it."

Moreover, the chances are high the selling party will enlist a professional negotiator's services too. If you go up against a professional who has likely negotiated countless deals, the chances of getting a deal that makes you happy are near zero.

Now, before you consider entering the negotiation process, you need to make sure you are looking at a deal worth pursuing or closing. You don't want to waste time or money on a deal that isn't even worth it in the first place.

With this in mind, here's a list of things to look for before concluding that a property is worth pursuing or entering the negotiation phase.

#1: A Good Location

The importance of location is not something that can be understated. A property in an unsuitable or poor location will never be a good investment.

As I mentioned in the subsection location, location, location, various factors will influence the desirability of a property's location. We looked at a number of them in a previous chapter.

As a quick recap, you want to make sure the following things check out:

- The crime rate in the area should be low.
- The local job market should be healthy and growing.
- The population should be steadily rising.
- Amenities like hospitals, fire stations, restaurants, and the like should be within reach.
- Public transportation facilities should be readily available.
- The area should be easily accessible and by multiple access roads instead of one.
- The area should not be prone to natural disasters like floods and earthquakes.

If all or most of these things check out, the property you have at hand has the markings of a great location.

#2: The listing price should be low

The property's listing or asking price should be below the fair market value, as determined by a professional appraisal discussed earlier. You always want to get a bargain on a property, no matter what the circumstances.

You should never consider paying more for a property than it is truly worth.

#3: The rental income should be high enough

You want a property that will produce a return which is high enough to pay for all expenses and still leave you with positive cash-flow. At the very least, you should be able to break even.

I know what you're asking, "Mas, how can I quickly assess this feature in a property I'm considering?"

Well, it's simple: *always follow the 1 percent rule of real estate.*

What is the 1 percent rule?

This rule states that properties that produce positive cash-flows have a monthly rent rate of at least 1 percent or greater than the purchase price. This rule will save you a lot of trouble; at the very least, it ensures that you will afford to pay your mortgage comfortably without having to dip into your pockets.

#4: Low operating costs

Expenses associated with the property you're thinking about purchasing must be reasonably low to provide a profit margin. If they are too high, they will eat into your rental income, and you could easily find yourself in the red.

Be sure to find a reasonable estimation of both fixed and variable expenses, and compare them against monthly income to establish that you are looking at a great deal.

#5: A high cap rate

A Cap Rate is the return on investment expected from purchasing a property. Here's another way to define a Cap Rate: the ratio of the Net Operating Income to the purchase price, expressed as a percentage.

Thus, to determine a properties Cap Rate, we use the following formula:

$$\text{Cap Rate} = \frac{\text{Net Operating Income} - \text{Expenses} \times 100\%}{\text{Purchase Price}}$$

Generally, real estate investors consider a Cap Rate of between 6 percent and 12 percent to be healthy. You are likely looking at a good deal if you determine that a property you are considering has a Cap Rate that falls within this range.

#6: Repair costs should be low

If you are looking at a property that needs repairs, you want to make sure that the cost of doing such repairs will not be massive; otherwise, you could find yourself in trouble. It comes down to what we discussed earlier.

When you take on a property with too many renovations, you will likely be looking at a development property, turning you into a speculator. As mentioned earlier, success with speculation requires that you know what you're doing. In other words, you need to be a professional who spends most of his time working in real estate and cutting deals for a living.

If you are not ready to become that person, only consider value-add properties that require a few minor and inexpensive repairs to reposition the property on the market.

#7: Appreciation

Last, you want to make sure you are purchasing a property whose value will likely appreciate.

Remember that in commercial real estate, you profit from monthly cash-flows and capital appreciation. A good property is one that will provide you an opportunity to profit from both ends.

How do you establish that?

That's simple: study historical property trends in the area. Have prices generally been falling or rising? That is the most accurate way to get your answer.

With this knowledge, you can now be confident of securing a great property deal. Now we'll talk about the acquisition process.

How to Navigate the Acquisition Process

I'll start our discussion about the acquisition process by noting something important.

Over the years, MarketSpace Capital has earned a reputation for having an entrepreneurial orientation. Rather than merely participating in business transactions with the sole goal of turning a profit, we take risks and solve problems so that we can add value.

We've managed to amass a huge database of acquaintances such as brokers, lenders, appraisers, co-development partners, landowners, etc. Given our business position, we consistently and literally get bombarded with countless investment opportunities.

However, because we have finite resources of time, people, capital, etc., we cannot afford to pursue every opportunity presented. We have had to find a way to separate the wheat from the chaff, before considering looking into a possible deal.

If a deal does not meet the minimum criteria, we immediately drop it from our consideration list long before it gobbles up more resources. On the other hand, when a deal pans out, we invest more resources to maximize its utility function.

Essentially, our business approach to investing in properties is systematic and well documented. We are more of a quant-based firm rather than a discretionary one.

Our systematic approach allows us to take disciplined action at every juncture, leaving little room for error. That is perhaps why we have successfully lived through many different economic cycles without suffering considerable losses in our portfolio.

Moreover, we keep fine-tuning our processes as we learn from past outcomes. Thus, our system makes it easy to capitalize on our experience and make adjustments that allow us to operate with even more efficiency.

That said, let me take you through our proven acquisition process to help you get a sense of how we run our core business.

Step #1: Deal Opportunity

As always, every deal usually begins with an invitation to participate in a specific deal. Sometimes, partners approach us directly at our headquarters, or dealer-makers contact any of our partners with a possible lead, which he or she makes available for our consideration.

Step #2: Acquisitions Team

Right out of the gate, the acquisitions team at the company receives the deal. They are in charge of receiving all external investment solicitations. They, in turn, pass the material over to the department heads. At this point, the opportunity goes through a quick perusal process to ascertain the opportunity's foundational nature.

At this stage, some of our key considerations are:

- The location. Does the property's location fit the description of a good location?
- Why type of property is it? Is it multifamily, single-family, a hotel, or mixed-use? Does it have a place in our portfolio?
- What timeframe are we working with here? Is the seller in a hurry?
- How much is the seller asking? Is it realistic?
- Why is the seller interested in selling the property? What is their motivation?
- What type of deal are they suggesting? Is it a joint venture?
- What is our perception of the involved market?
- What alternative uses does the property have?
- What are the zoning restrictions associated with the property?
- What are the advantages and disadvantages associated with this deal? Do the upsides justify the downsides?

If a deal does not meet the minimum requirements based on our well-laid-out criteria, we quickly abandon the idea before it further consumes our resources. On the other hand, if the deal passes this initial test, it will proceed to the next step in the process.

Step #3: Deal review

The deal review stage is where we do most of the real homework on a possible deal. Compared to the quick perusal done previously to ascertain the bare minimums, the deal review process is a lot more comprehensive.

The deal review phase involves the following processes:

1: Site assessment

First, the work begins with a site assessment.

The person or people involved in this kind of work will look at the property and assess the following areas:

- What is the property's address/location?
- What zoning restrictions has the local government imposed in the area?
- How well is that market doing? What conditions prevail?
- What is the highest and best use of the property?
- What is the current condition of comparable properties, and how much are they selling/renting for in the current market?
- What type of consultants will be needed to perform a further assessment of this property? At a minimum, we often require engineers, architects, commercial building inspectors, and financial analysts.
- What environmental concerns does the property have, and how do they affect our liability?
- Does the topography of the area suit the intended project?
- What strengths or weaknesses do we perceive in that market?

2: Consultant assessment

The next step involves a consultant assessment of the building or property.

This step is crucial because our company consistently invests in value-add and development properties. Therefore, we need the input of a professional who will examine the property and establish its actual condition.

The consultant is typically a company with an in-house team of engineers, architects, financial analysts, commercial building inspectors, and other professionals, who will work together to prepare a report that paints an accurate picture of the property, its condition and possible renovations costs.

This report, also called Property Condition Report, will be handy and required down the road by other parties such as insurers, lenders, and government agencies to guide their decision-making process, making this a crucial step in the process. It can also assist in the overall price negotiation with the seller.

3: Market conditions

Next, we conduct a market condition analysis. This step aims to uncover the nature of the market, vis-à-vis the property's location.

We make it a point to explore the following areas:

- What demographic segment are we looking at? Who is the primary target market?
- Are there barriers to entry? What are they? Does it have to do with the cost?
- What role has the seller partaken in that market so far?
- Is there room for growth in this market, or is it already established?
- Are amenities like schools, shopping centers, restaurants, etc. within reach?
- What is the nature of comparative properties in the area? What is their condition, age, and selling price?
- What are the housing statistics in the area? Does it sound like there is a need?
- Can the property be described as the highest and best use?
- What are some of the costs, rates, or terms associated with previously closed deals, and how well do they fit within the objectives pursued?

4: Cost projections

In this step, we look at the hard data to estimate the project's expected cost and the potential profit we can estimate to reap from the project. In other words, this is a feasibility analysis.

We sometimes outsource this process to a well-trained financial analyst who will look at the current numbers from the property, the probable costs of development, and the estimated costs of financing the deal.

Here is what we typically want:

- Estimating consultant fees
- Suggestions on improving the odds of success
- Suggestions on avoidable costs
- Identification and estimation of the downside risks
- When that is the objective, the analyst will also estimate the expected profit from the property's sale.

5: Market head discussion

In this step, the market head will go over the details of the deal made available by the reports to establish whether it is viable and how easy it shall be to position the property in its market.

Some pertinent things that the market head looks at include the following:

- Based on the information uncovered, is this project a good investment?
- Are there any overlooked concepts that ought to become part of our considerations?
- What things need more consideration when performing due diligence?
- The amount of time needed to conduct due diligence.

Once done, the market head will provide a narrative report on the whole project.

Step #4: Terms and timing

At this point, the company proceeds to draft an initial offer on the property. The offer gets reviewed by the company's Investment Committee.

The things covered here include:

- The terms, the conditions, and the timing regarding the deal the company is willing to accept.
- What options the company will use to acquire the property. Will it go with a direct purchase, buy with a takedown, or seller financing?

At this stage, we also consider a legal review of the offer vital.

Step #5: Offer and engagement/deal presentation

At this juncture, the team prepares a summary of the deal and presents it to the department heads, the investment committee and the company's attorney.

If the decision among all these parties is unanimous, the summary is signed off.

Next, the execution of the deal terms takes place. That usually entails the attorney preparing documents such as the Letter Of Intent (LOI), the purchase contract/joint venture contract, and other required documents.

If the decision-makers aren't satisfied at this point, then one of two things will happen:

- The team may have to conduct more research to uncover more facts, or the deal terms undergo a modification process.
- The deal gets rejected, with the seller notified of the same.

Step #6: Deal approved

Once a deal is approved, the contract and the Letter of Intent proceed with the deal's timing.

At this point, we may bring in a consultant to negotiate the deal terms on our behalf. Also, abstract documents for critical dates and deal tracking are drafted.

Step #7: Critical dates/due diligence

In this phase we do the following:

- Notify the title company of our involvement and serve them with the contract documents
- Work closely with the title company to address objections
- Perform the due diligence on the property
- Obtain abstract documents for deal terms on critical dates, reporting, and tracking
- Receive tracking reports from our consultants who have undertaken the due diligence process
- Review the due diligence reports conducted with an appropriate team before closing

Step #8: Deal closing

Deal closing is the final step. Here, we finalize all the deal's details and acquire the property in question.

Various things play out during this step. They include:

- Working with legal to go over all the paperwork associated with closing
- Contacting the title company and inform them of the closing date
- Providing the title company with the relevant closing documents
- Obtaining the electronic version of the closing book

Now you have intimate knowledge of how we conduct the acquisition process from start to finish.

Without a doubt, as you have seen, the process is comprehensive, but when putting massive amounts of capital into deals the way we do at MarketSpace Capital, we've got to be as comprehensive as possible. After all, due diligence could be the difference between profitable real estate investing or something short of profits!

Now that we're talking about due diligence …

How to Conduct the Due Diligence Process

Before you can acquire a property, you have to engage in proper due diligence. Due diligence is the kind of extra homework needed on a property to verify that all claims made by the seller are factual. As an old Russian proverb goes, "Trust, but verify."

Doing this is vital because sellers often misrepresent some facts and bend certain truths about their property that could be quite costly to the buyer. You want to protect yourself and your lender by ensuring you conduct a proper background check on a property before you acquire it.

Now, something worth noting is that due diligence often takes place just after you've placed a property under your control by signing a contract. The contract document should contain a clause that specifies the due diligence period. This clause allows you to specify the number of days needed to conduct due diligence before your earnest money deposit becomes at risk or finalizing matters on the deal.

You should take practically everything the seller says about the property with a grain of salt until you can find proof. As someone once said, "The seller is guilty until proven innocent."

Issues uncovered during the due diligence should provide grounds for renegotiation of terms or even contract termination if they happen to be too serious and risky. As you can see, due diligence helps alleviate many concerns that will stop you from entering into a bad deal simply because you couldn't verify the facts.

That brings us to this all-important question: "Mas, what should I check when conducting due diligence?"

First, realize that due diligence can be costly. Conducting a comprehensive due diligence process can cost thousands upon thousands of dollars. Therefore, you want to save yourself some costs right off the bat if you can, unless the deal looks quite promising.

I know what you're thinking, "Mas, how can I do that?"

The first thing you need to do is use some of the cheap options made available to you earlier in the book. This way, you can get an initial picture of what may lurk underneath the surface.

Next, I would recommend using the Due Diligence Checklist that we use at MarketSpace Capital. It is a detailed list that has been developed, refined, and expended over many years. I have included the high-level checklist later in this chapter, and I hope it can help you as you continue to determine if you should, or should not, move forward on an investment.

From there, it will simply be a matter of gut-feeling your way through it. You'll consistently ask yourself, "Does this feel right, or should I just drop everything now when I can?"

Next you will need to ...

#1: Conduct a quick check on the property

The first thing you can do is show up at the premises for a quick glance at the property. Is the location good? What's the property's condition? Are you comfortable with that? You might even want to seek the opinion of a competent property manager on this matter.

#2: Get a title commitment

After conducting a quick first-glance look at the property, the next thing is to order a title commitment from a title company. This request will prompt the company to conduct a title search.

Your goal is to determine how easy it will be to acquire title to the property. If multiple issues appear during the process of requesting a title commitment, issues that make it hard for you to move quickly with the process, then you should smell a rat and should reconsider your options.

Some possible issues that should raise concerns include:

- Tax liens
- Access problems
- Restrictions

- Encumbrances
- Easements
- Divorce decrees
- Court orders
- Probate issues

#3: Take a quick look at the numbers

A third option is to take a look at the property's numbers. The numbers always tell a story about what is truly going on under the bed.

Remember, your primary investment goal is to make money. Therefore, you want to be sure that the property you are investing in will do a stellar job of generating revenue. If it is a money-pit, you will want to dump it as fast as you possibly can.

To make sure the numbers are right, you will have to obtain all the financial statements, receipts, and anything else the seller makes available. From there, you will want a professional accountant experienced in commercial real estate to cross-check and audit them. The accountant should crunch the numbers for you and point out any discrepancies that would raise eyebrows.

Does the property produce the cash-flow advertised? What about the expenses? Are they in-line with what you were told, or do they deviate? And if they do, by how much?

At this point, you should have a gut idea or feeling of whether things feel right. If so, you can proceed with the other more expensive options down the line. If they don't, you can opt-out, saving yourself time and money.

If your preliminary checks produce good enough results, you may opt to go on with the rest of the process.

Proceeding with the Process

This process goes deep and will often involve professionals. You may even want to hire a company specializing in this kind of work. In many cases, you will spend weeks, even months on this process.

For your convenience, here's the checklist we use at MarketSpace Capital to conduct due diligence at the end of this discussion. You can either use it as it is or customize it to fit your needs. The list is quite long and definitive, but all your checks will generally fall under three categories.

1: Physical

The physical checks are some of the most important ones to conduct, and you will need professionals to conduct them.

Problems that come up during these checks tend to be among the most difficult to discover, but they can be truly devastating. Their impact on the value of the property can be quite substantial.

Checklist items under the physical category include:

- Planning
- Consultants
- Utilities
- Soil survey/Topography
- Site work
- Drainage/Grading
- Traffic engineering/Roadways & Railways/Access

2: Financial

The quick financial exercise you carried out earlier notwithstanding, it's imperative go even deeper and examine more material. There is a cost item on the list, but you should work with your accountant to factor in the following as well:

- Income and expense statements

- Tax returns
- Rent rolls
- Utility bills
- Property tax bills

PLEASE NOTE: You must never short-cut this step or try to handle this section of due diligence personally or on your own, no matter how good you think you are with numbers. Get experienced professional help and pay for it!

3: Legal

Last, you have the legal category of checks.

Here too, enlisting professional help is essential. An attorney will work together with a title and an escrow company to get most of the work here done.

The key things examined here include:

- Issues regarding the survey as well as the title
- Potential environmental concerns associated with the property
- Encroachment and improper special uses associated with the property

These are issues that could put you in real trouble if overlooked. In many cases, such issues could imply a deal's termination.

Items on the legal checklist include:

- Permit requirements
- Environmental
- Legal/closing/easements/right-of-way

Now, you could have other categories that cover issues you deem important. However, at MarketSpace Capital we feel that you will hardly go wrong if you cover these three basic categories comprehensively.

Let's spend some time talking about something that many people do not consider: the time to buy and sell real estate.

When to Buy and When to Sell

Not all periods throughout a given year are equal, especially when you are seeking a single-family residential investment property. Deals will tend to favor the buy or sell-side at different times, and you would be wise to factor in that reality as you plan your entry and exit strategies.

If you are buying, you probably want to get the biggest discount you can get. On the other hand, if you are selling, you want to get the highest possible price possible.

Here's the good news: The real estate market follows a pattern of seasonality, which tends to affect supply and demand parameters. You will undoubtedly have to go against the crowd if you hope to profit from this cycle.

Here's what I mean.

During the winter season, few people want to strike deals. Most people prefer being indoors and perform basic tasks like going to work, then head straight home afterward.

What does this imply?

Most people will not be looking to shop for real estate. Those who do will be in the minority, meaning there's a guarantee there will be a short supply of buyers in the market. That should be good news for you because you can push for a bargain.

Another thing to consider is that people who list properties during winter are probably in a hurry to sell and will likely be interested in negotiating and cutting deals.

Think about it. Most people don't wish to do much during winter, and if someone lists a property on the market, that should tell you something—the person is selling because they need to. Otherwise, they would just wait for better conditions. Thus, shopping for property deals when everyone else is not in the mood to do so is the key to buying cheap, and winter is a great time to do that.

The opposite is true when you join the selling side. You don't want to be listing anything when buyers are few and far between. You will likely meet savvy buyers interested in cutting the price down to the bone since they think you're desperate to sell, a position you never want to be in at any time as an investor.

Remember, you are looking for the best exit price possible. What better time to sell than when buyers have filled the market and are trying to outdo each other? That is a good time to lock in a great price.

You should be looking to sell during the summer. That's right—when everyone is in a good mood and outgoing. During such times, the odds tip in your favor.

Summertime presents a virtual bubble period. During this season, there is such great demand for real estate that it often triggers bidding wars among buyers. They will often feel incentivized to quote the highest price possible for fear that other lined-up buyers could get the deal; what a great time to be a seller!

When to buy and sell boils down to timing the seasons and doing the opposite of what the majority does.

Now, supply and demand patterns may not always pronounce themselves so well that it guarantees a fortune. That is especially true considering that other factors could also be at play, such as the local market's overall nature.

That notwithstanding, at MarketSpace Capital, we believe that if you are a skilled negotiator, or hire one, you should get better deals by following this basic principle.

We've talked about Cap Rates before, and at this point you have a good idea of what they are.

As promised, let's take a deeper look into them to uncover how important they can be.

Cap Rates 101: A Complete Understanding

First off, you understand that a cap rate is a property's net operating income ratio to its selling price, expressed as a ratio. A glance at the Cap Rate gives you a bit of information about the kind of return you can expect on your investment.

Here's something else you need to know: A cap rate also gives you an idea of how long it will take for the net operating produced by the property to recapitalize the asset's full value. Let me explain.

If, for instance, you have a property with a cap rate of 4 percent, it means you are going to earn a 4 percent return on your money once you invest. It also means that it will take 25 years for the property to pay for itself fully and become debt-free. In other words, dividing 100 by the cap rate will give you an idea of how long it takes to recapitalize the asset's value. That is useful information to have as you think about where to direct your money.

A cap rate can also help you estimate whether a project is safe and makes sense or whether you should just cut and run.

How?

Calculating a Project's Viability

To begin, it helps to understand that we can classify cap rates into two:

- Entry Cap Rate
- Exit Cap Rate

These terms are self-explanatory. An Entry Cap Rate is what you get (your rate) when you enter a property deal, while an Exit Cap Rate is what you get (your rate) when you exit a property deal. If you can get an idea of the values of both, you can calculate the project's viability.

Example

Let's say you run into a shopping center with a net operating income of $1,000,000 and an Entry Cap Rate of 5.5 percent. When you do the math, right out of the gate you know that the property is worth $18,181,181.

Let's consider this to be a class B property, and you have an idea of how you could transform it into a Class A property, with a bit of renovation, then you can increase the rents. The Cap Rates in the Class A market are 5 percent, and you know that your exit rate will be the same.

You also know that your net operating income from raising rents will go up to 1,400,000. From that, you calculate that your renovation improvements will result in your property being worth $28,000,000 ($1.4 million divided by 5 percent).

Now you know that your deal has a profit margin of $10,000,000, but you haven't factored in the renovation costs, which are likely to be about $6,000,000.

You are now aware that you will likely pocket a profit of $4,000,000 just from renovating the project, increasing the rents, and improving the property from a Class B to a Class A and later selling it.

NOTE: This is an oversimplified example that leaves many factors out of the equation, and should not be taken as an actual case. These factors could make the calculations a lot more complicated than they appear to be here. The point is to highlight how useful cap rates knowledge can be.

What factors affect cap rates?

A property's location, occupancy rate, and physical condition happen to be the most critical factors that affect the highs and lows of a Cap Rate. The higher a piece of property is on the desirability scale, the lower the cap rate and vice versa.

This now gets a bit more interesting.

Often, naïve investors make the mistake of assuming that the higher the Cap Rate, the better a deal is as a whole. Many assume that a higher Cap Rate means a higher return rate on investment and a low recapitalization period.

In a way, that's true. However, things are never quite that simple in real estate.

The reality is that the higher the Cap Rate, the higher the perceived risk in the situation. Often, properties with high cap rates require major overhauls that involve the infusion of large amounts of capital just to make them operational and more marketable.

Low cap rates are usually common with investment-grade properties that require little to no additional work, such as Class A properties.

Usually, it's a matter of risk appetite, appreciation of the work involved, and experience that dictates one's preference of properties with a certain level of cap rates.

Whatever you do, if you are new, risk-averse, and looking to invest passively in real estate, never just jump into opportunities with higher cap rates. Often, you will just want to latch onto a Class A property that comes with a correspondingly lower Cap Rate.

Name_____

Address _____

℞ CHAPTER FIVE
NETWORK BUILDING 101
HOW TO IDENTIFY AND BUILD RELATIONSHIPS WITH THIRD-PARTY CONTRACTORS

Refills_____

M.D _____

"Networking is an essential part of building wealth."
Armstrong Williams, American political commentator,
entrepreneur, and bestselling author

"I was born in the US to Japanese immigrants, grew up in New York and never once felt or saw the effects of discrimination due to my culture. I moved back to Tokyo for 7 years during the 80s, and living in Japan as an American born person, I felt like I had to make various compromises with the culture, and had to try harder just to make friends, have fun, and get good grades. This relocation forced me to be more outgoing, which is a character trait I have to this day. In short, I never meet a stranger!"
Dr. Masaki Oishi, Real Estate Investor

No matter how good you feel you are at finding and investing in good deals, you can never hope to work alone. There's just too much work to do and you can never be a jack of all trades. A typical real estate transaction involves several steps and processes, all of which require expert knowledge.

Therefore, even if you mastered the entire process, there would still be gaps in your knowledge regarding some critical areas, and mistakes in these key areas often lead to failure.

The point I'm trying to make here is simple: Ensure you surround yourself with several third-party service providers who are better than you, and can help make the whole process easier to accomplish. Remember that going into this business as a lone ranger will get you a metaphorical bullet in the head (losses).

Based on my years of investing in real estate, I will point out the kind of relationships that have formed the backbone of my success. You may need to expand this list depending on your situation, but as I've mentioned in other areas, think of this list as the required minimum for passive investors.

1: Property managers

The first class of people you will want to consider are property managers.

These professionals take the burden of managing your property off your shoulders. A good property manager should be able to perform a list of duties that include, but are not limited to:

- Advertising the property to the public to get tenants
- Collecting rents on your behalf
- Managing payments to your lender
- Handling tenant requests
- Handling tenant eviction process as well as lawsuits
- Handling repair and maintenance

- Taxes payment
- Vetting tenants
- Advising you on rental prices
- Managing garbage collection and cleaning

Once you have a property under your name, property managers make the idea of passive income a reality.

You can locate a competent property manager by conducting a simple keyword search through a search engine of your choosing. You may also consult with other known acquaintances in the business for a referral.

2: Lawyers and accountants

Real estate attorneys will help with the legal aspects of a property transaction. A good real estate attorney will:

- Help draft closing documents
- Review the closing paperwork to make sure they are in line with your interests
- Insure you are gaining clean title to the property
- Manage emergent disputes between you and the seller
- Represent you in court in the event of a legal issue
- Identify legal issues regarding the property you intend to purchase
- Oversee or transfer funds on your behalf

Real estate accountants are just as important. Among the most important roles a real estate accountant will play include:

- Filling your taxes in a way that allows you to take advantage of deductions in the most efficient way possible
- Advising you on what tax-advantaged investments decisions to consider
- Performing financial background checks on possible deals to uncover the real truth

- Advising you on how to leverage your investments safely to avoid probable bankruptcy

- Helping you locate other competent professionals and partners to work with based on your investment endeavors

The best way to hire worthy real estate attorneys and accountants is through referrals, since reputation and service quality tend to be key factors in judging quality.

3: Brokers/Agents

Brokers and agents act as intermediaries in the business of transacting real estate. A broker has had more training and is more knowledgeable and experienced than a real estate agent.

If you have never transacted real estate, you most certainly need a broker or agent. People often make the mistake of cutting costs by sacrificing the option of hiring these professionals. That is a grave mistake.

Whether you are on the buying or selling side, hiring and paying brokers and agents is essential; it allows you to tap into their collective knowledge, experience and skills.

For instance, a competent broker has developed negotiation skills that would take months or years to learn. Additionally, brokers/agents have first-hand market knowledge. Since they get involved in closing many deals, they can advise you about a property's likely or ideal price. This knowledge can serve as a useful basis for the negotiation process.

Brokers can also negotiate for other services such as inspection, appraisals, repairs, and so on. You could easily get into a bad deal just by not seeking their services.

Once again, the best way to access good talent in this area is to get a referral.

4: Current owners

Always foster great relationships with the current owners of the properties you're thinking of investing in at any given point. Whether land or buildings, someone currently owns the property you want to invest in, and having a good relationship with them is essential.

I know what you're wondering, "Mas, how do I form relationships with the current owners?"

Well, it's simple.

Make it your business to know them to the best of your ability and understand their interests. You could invite them for coffee or lunch and strike up a casual, friendly conversation about their family and friends, their passions, journey into investing in real estate, and the reasons motivating the property's sale.

Even when the current owner has a third-party representative like a real estate agent, never close a deal without knowing the seller on a personal level. You could gain an advantage you might not get anywhere else.

People often mistakenly conclude that real estate is all about negotiating deals like unemotional robots, closing them and moving on. This kind of attitude does work for some people some of the time, but ultimately, real estate is highly personal; it's about creating and nurturing relationships.

Sometimes, you may run into a seller who wants to make a deal with a buyer who shares their passion for the property. Sometimes you find that someone has a pressing need to exit, and they wish they could find someone to strike a deal with as quickly as possible.

In any event, getting to know people will provide you with insights on how to serve their needs best and secure a great deal in the process. You would do well to make it your business to cultivate a warm personality and genuine interest in knowing people.

5: Construction companies

Do you want to invest in value-add and development properties? Well then, you will need to find a reliable construction company you can work with on your projects. The same is also important if you hope to develop properties from scratch.

A construction company will cost-effectively help bring your ideas to life because they have the knowledge, experience and business contacts. They can also assist you in the value engineering along the way.

The good thing about finding a construction company to work with is that once you find one that makes you happy, you can always patronize the same company every time you need their kind of service.

There are many ways you can hire a construction company. If you have a big project, you can advertise an invitation to tender and evaluate bids. If you have a small renovation project, you can inquire among your contacts and ask for a referral and a quote.

6: Co-sponsors/GPs

Co-sponsors/GPs have to be the most critical party you will ever deal with, if you want to be a passive real estate investor.

A co-sponsor, also called a general partner (GP), refers to the company or sponsor that invests money contributed as equity or by limited partners in real estate investments.

In other words, a general partner carries the responsibility of bringing an investment project to fruition. A general partner researches the deal, performs the necessary due diligence, arranges for financing, secures contractors, and generally does everything else that limited partners won't do.

That is the role that we play at MarketSpace Capital. We help investors who wish to passively participate in commercial real estate realize their dream. We pool funds from investors and use them to acquire revenue-generating properties.

You need to know how to select a good general partner. To do so, you must ask yourself some basic questions and have ready answers before you jump in.

Those questions include but are not limited to:

- Does this sponsor have much experience in the local market?

- How experienced is the sponsor in handling investments in this asset class? If so, do they have a track record to back up their claims?

- What losing streaks does this sponsor have, and how bad were the losses? Were they so severe that they financially hurt the investors?

- How well aware does this sponsor seem to be about the risks involved in what they are doing, and does their plan to manage them sound prudent?

- Does this sponsor have a well-documented system of doing business, or do they seem to approach their decisions in an ad hoc manner?

You can add your own criteria to this mix, but remember that whatever you do, a proven track-record documenting performance in both good and bad markets is essential.

Evaluating Bids: A Simple How-To

Some instances will call on you to solicit potential suppliers by putting out an invitation to tender, something that may be especially true in a case when you are procuring an expensive service or goods supply. For instance, construction is an expensive project. It also requires a high degree of specialization. Problems in this area can make or break your project.

Let's say you cannot find reliable prospects through referrals sent your way. In that case, you may benefit from advertising an invitation to tender. You can lay out the terms of your commitment and the exact qualities you demand from such a contractor and then sit and wait for proposals or bids to roll in.

Once you have the bid, what should you do next?

Well, you should apply the criteria you deem best to select several suitable candidates to negotiate with, ensuring you get the best deal possible. The candidate who provides the best offering (not just price and terms) during negotiation wins the contract. This is truly one of the most stable methods for finding contractors or suppliers to work with on your projects. However, it's worth noting that your evaluation criterion is what counts the most. Although there is no magical template, it helps to know which factors will likely affect your decision-making process.

Most selection processes rely on the following criteria:

- The lowest price of all offers made by contenders
- The most economically advantageous tender
- The quality of the proposed solution
- The most experienced bidder
- The median value
- Disregard of the extremes

It is up to you to come up with the selection criteria that best fits your needs. As stated before, there can be no one-size-fits-all selection process that works for everybody.

Next up, we'll talk about how to structure deals.

Name _____

Address _____

R CHAPTER SIX

STRUCTURING THE DEAL

Refills _____

M.D _____

"The first one gets the oyster; the second gets the shell."

Andrew Carnegie, Scottish-American industrialist
and steel mogul

"I used to think that I knew everything. But as I aged—and made mistakes in life—I realized that I needed to surround myself with people that were better, smarter and more experienced than myself. Always ... always ... always ... seek professional advice, even if you think you already know the answers because often times you will find that you don't."

Dr. Masaki Oishi, Real Estate Investor

Investing in real estate is a capital-intensive operation where only a few people can afford to go at it alone, and even those with tremendous means at their disposal would love to minimize their risk exposure. Therefore, real estate deals that involve multiple parties are quite essential. As you can guess, there are many ways of structuring real estate transactions in a way that makes them beneficial to all involved parties.

This chapter will explore some of the popular ways of structuring deals. The aim is to ensure you stay informed of all the various ways you could get involved in deals even without being massively capitalized.

Different Debt Structures in Commercial Investments

One of the most popular ways of making real estate deals work is by financing them using debt.

Debt is straightforward. You simply borrow money from some entity such as a bank, credit union, mortgage lender, insurance company, pension fund, private debt fund and so on. You agree to pay back the money over time and at a specific interest rate.

Even individuals have the chance to provide debt financing. For instance, when a company issues a corporate bond, and the public buys that bond, they are, in essence, the company's debt investors. Debt investors can exist in real estate as well.

Debt financing poses the least amount of risk both to the company and the lender. For one thing, debt investors have a priority claim on a business's assets if they don't get paid. If a business went bankrupt today, debtors would have a priority claimant status and every right under the law to go after that business's assets to pay themselves first.

On the other hand, debt financing poses less appreciation risk to the business itself because debt investors have no equity claim. Debt investors will never take an ownership stake in a business. That means they can't influence critical decision-making processes.

You also rid yourself of the burden of having to pay them a dividend out of profits.

That said, there are two types of real estate debt.

1: Senior secured or unsubordinated debt

For the most part, mortgages make up this debt class. It is worth noting that this kind of debt involves the least amount of risk to the lender or investor.

The first reason for this is the property under question gets attached as collateral through a mortgage or deed of trust, thus the name "secured loan."

The second reason is this type of debt gets classified as a first lien, meaning the lender who provides financing gets paid first in the event of asset liquidation due to default.

Now, given that the risk associated with this form of financing is minimal, the returns are minimal. Banks and other lenders who participate in this kind of lending earn the least amount of interest on their invested dollars.

2: Mezzanine or subordinated debt

The next class of debt is mezzanine debt, a form of debt that carries more risk than senior secured debt. Payment of senior secured debt usually comes as a priority, before the mezzanine debt, in the event of necessary liquidation.

The second reason is that mezzanine debt is often under-secured, meaning this debt has more downside risk.

The good thing with mezzanine debt is that it often offers the chance for the lender to also take an equity position as a sweetener, or "equity kicker." Equity positions are usually more desirable in terms of returns earned on invested capital.

Another desirable feature of mezzanine debt is that returns are comparatively higher. The median rate ranges are usually 8 percent to 14 percent when combining the interest rate, as well as the equity kicker.

The high yield combined with consistent monthly or quarterly payments makes this debt class a proper fit for conservative investors who want a predictable cash flow yet are seeking a higher return than a senior-secured lender.

Issuing (Raising) equity

Deals can also have an equity offerings structure; equity is an ownership stake in a business.

Equity financing is the riskiest form of funding for all parties. An equity position is risky because, from an investor's perspective, they are the most junior in the claimant status, and get the last claim on the assets should a business go under or file for bankruptcy, as opposed to the debt investors, which get paid first.

Additionally, the value of your equity holdings gets marked to market, which means it can rise and fall according to the prevailing market conditions. In a bad economy, equity investors suffer the most.

Nevertheless, there are also considerable upsides to being an equity investor. For one thing, equity investors get the lion's share of the profits from a successful venture. If the venture does well, the return on capital also tends to be the highest.

Equity financing can fall into the following classification.

1: Preferred equity

New equity holders mostly favor this type of equity financing. They assume virtually the same level of risk as any equity investor. The main difference is that they get to claim assets first until they reach their targeted amount before other, more junior (common) equity investors claim the rest.

The downside is that the return on investment is lower since they take on a lower risk. These investors also get limited voting rights on the core decisions regarding the business.

2: Common equity

This type of financing is usually made available by existing equity holders such as owners, early investors, developers, limited partners, etc. It is the riskiest undertaking because investors in this class get the last claim on assets should a venture or business fail or fail to meet its debt obligations.

The upside is that common equity investors usually pocket the most money from an operation's generated profits.

As you can see, there is room for everyone, depending on risk tolerance and appetite for gains. You have to work out in which part of the equation you want to participate.

Alternative Structure – Opportunity Zone

Deals can also adopt a structure revolving around opportunity zones.

If you've never heard of them, opportunity zones are areas deemed underdeveloped and therefore economically distressed.

The President and congressional members invented opportunity zones in 2017 when the Tax and Jobs Act came into effect. The whole idea was to incentivize investors to risk capital in these areas and boost their economic outlook.

Even though investing in opportunity zones sounds like a noble and patriotic idea, why should anyone do it? Why should investing in an underdeveloped area be attractive? Why risk your money? After all, I've previously mentioned the importance of investing based on location, location, location in well-developed markets, especially if you are not ready for a wild ride that could lead to bankruptcy. If you are an investor who abhors risky situations, underdeveloped markets should be the last thing in your mind.

Investing in opportunity zones is desirable because of the unique tax benefits offered. Investors can receive preferential tax treatment that could enhance their bottom-line. One advantage relates to tax exclusion and another has to do with tax deferment.

I am sure you will agree that tax is one of the heaviest burdens for anyone who makes a lot of money. No one likes to pay Uncle Sam all those dollars. Any high paying tax rates certainly dampens your ability to build wealth.

When you look at it that way, investing in opportunity zones looks like a great idea, and it sounds great to many people since estimates show that a record $75 billion has been invested in opportunity zones thus far.

With that kind of influx, it is improbable that you will be looking at a terrible risk. You can think of these areas as emerging markets. Investor activity will likely boost the availability of amenities in such an area, which can further work in your favor.

One of the easiest ways for an individual to invest in an opportunity zone is through an opportunity fund, a fund like any other that participates in opportunity zones. It can be in the form of a corporation or a partnership. An opportunity fund has the allowance to take advantage of the tax benefit only if it meets the minimum requirements.

First, the fund needs to own at least 90 percent of its assets originating from its chosen opportunity zones. Second, if the fund invests in property, it needs to renovate the property substantially within 30 months before it can qualify for the said tax benefits.

Substantially, in this case, means that the fund needs to invest an equal amount of money in a property as it did during acquisition. Therefore, if I acquire property priced at $300,000, I will need to put in an extra $300,000 within 30 months before I qualify for the tax benefits.

Another significant advantage of investing in opportunity zones is that despite the documented tax benefits, the longer you hold on to a property, the lower your tax burden becomes.

For instance, if you hold on to a real estate/property investment for five years, your burden goes down by 10 percent. If you stick around for seven years, your burden goes down by 15 percent. If you stay with your holdings for ten years without exiting, you owe no tax on the fund's appreciation.

It is worth noting that there are opportunity zones in all fifty states. All you need to do to get involved is to find a fund with great potential and invest with it.

Alternative Structure – Public-Private Partnership

Another standard deal structure is Public-Private Partnerships. As the name suggests, these partnerships involve both the public and private sectors working together to achieve a common goal.

The public often gets cynical about these kinds of partnerships mainly because such arrangements can sometimes have conflicts of interest, corruption, rent-seeking and added taxpayer burden. However, the truth is that such partnerships have existed for many generations and have been instrumental in quality government service provision to the public.

For instance, if a government wants to provide water services to its local population, it may lack the specialty skills required to render such a service while adhering to safety standards. In such a case, the government may find it beneficial to partner with a private firm equipped with the necessary expertise and resources.

The same thing happens in real estate. There are particular construction or improvement projects that the government cannot, or should not, handle on its own. In such cases, the government will opt to strike a deal with a company equipped with relevant experience in the area.

The beauty of such partnerships is that the overall outcome much better and risk exposure is reduced. Instead of going alone into a construction project of, say, a school, you can partner with a solvent party that helps you split your risk appropriately.

The good thing is that governments usually have a number of structuring options they can use to finance projects involving public-private partnerships. Here are a few of these options.

1: Tax Increment Financing (TIF)

TIFs primary design objective is to help governments revitalize areas (or districts) that have fallen behind economically. The idea is that by investing in redevelopment and infrastructure, these areas will become more attractive to private investors.

To make TIFs work, the government usually forgoes the collection of increased future tax revenues for a specified period. That puts the government in a position where the TIF can issue bonds purchased by the public or some entity such as a bank, and the taxes paid by the developer are used to finance the project involved in the partnership.

The presupposition is the estimated tax increments the government decided to forego will pay off the bonds.

2: Payment In Lieu Of Taxes (PILOTs)

This form of financing works almost the same way TIFs. By this, I mean this form of financing hinges upon anticipated revenues.

The only difference is the revenue anticipated here is not tax revenue in a technical sense but revenue from a tax-exempt entity. This money gets paid to the local government to offset losses brought about by non-payment of tax, which is usually the case with a non-taxable property such as Federal Land and Public Universities.

The PILOT payments made by such entities help sustain the local government and encourage it to keep providing essential services to the local communities. The local government can issue bonds backed by such payments and can use them to fund development projects.

3: Public Improvement Districts (PIDs)

Financing can also come from Public Improvement Districts, which are special entities existing in particular areas with the lawful mandate to levy special taxes on local properties. The tax revenues collected then get used to improve the local area. That places these organizations in a position to issue debt and finance local public projects such as bridges, drainage improvements, water systems, sidewalks, streets, wastewater lines, etc.

4: Community Development Block Grants (CDBG)

These are grants that originate from the Department of Housing and Urban Development (HUD). They are provided annually to local governments for infrastructure development, anti-poverty programs, affordable housing programs, etc. The amount allocated to each government depends on a proprietary formula.

5: Tax-Exempt Financing

Tax-exempt financing is another powerful tool at the government's disposal. It is particularly viable in areas designated as economically inferior.

The basic idea is to issue near tax-free bonds to the public. "Near tax-free" is main incentive that may make these securities attractive to public investors. The dividend and interest earned on such bonds will not incur federal or state taxes.

This form of financing is an attractive option for the government that opts to use it because the interest paid on such bonds is usually lower than other taxable securities. In essence, it is borrowing on the cheap. The government can then turn around use this money to finance public development projects.

6: Tax credits

Tax credits have a design structure meant to reduce the amount of tax owed to the local or federal government. By reducing the amount of tax payable, it reduces an investor's downside risk.

Tax credits can take many forms and can be used to incentivize investors to use private equity to finance development projects. One such example is the Low-Income Housing Tax Credit, which encourages investors to construct properties that provide affordable housing in the U.S. There are also many others.

7: Environmental grants/underwriting

There is also the option of government-sponsored grants or offers to underwrite environmentally friendly projects. That is especially true if you factor in green space in your project or intend to protect and maintain wildlife habitat. By providing such incentives, the risk perceived by the investor decreases.

As we've said, public-private partnerships provide a win-win scenario for both parties and should be an attractive consideration for any company that participates in real estate. At MarketSpace Capital, we actively seek out such opportunities due to their low-risk nature and have participated in several of them.

In the next chapter, we will look at emerging architecture trends that improve land use.

Name_____

Address_____

R CHAPTER SEVEN

MODERN FORMS OF ARCHITECTURE THAT IMPROVE LAND USE

Refills_____

M.D _____

"...We must continually reinvent ourselves, responding to changing times with innovative new business models."

Akira Mori, real estate developer and CEO, Mori Trust

"If I were to go back in time and give advice to my 20-year-old self, I would encourage myself to stay more focused and engaged with all of the investment opportunities that are out there. Understand that investing may start small, but the principal amount can quickly compound and grow; the sooner you start, the faster it can build in value. I would also have looked at career opportunities differently. Instead of accepting the NIH Scholarship for medical training, perhaps I should have followed my dreams of joining the US Navy first, and then gone into medical school. After all, isn't the US Navy a great way to see the world?"

Dr. Masaki Oishi, Real Estate Investor

This chapter focuses on architectural styles and urban design that make the most use of available land.

You see, productive land is a scarce resource. You can make more of almost everything else, but you cannot make more land. This is especially the case when you are investing in urban or suburban areas, which, without a doubt, are the most lucrative markets for investment with minimal downside risk.

Trends show that more and more people, especially the younger generation, keep migrating to urban areas to search for employment opportunities. Additionally, there seems to be a preference for the perks of urban livelihood among the young generation. Thus, urban and suburban areas are in higher demand than ever before, and any smart person would be wise to put their money in such areas.

The problem with these locations is there is little room for improvement, and little available land is expensive. Thus, as an investor, should you have such land, you have to make the wisest use of the available land, which means adopting building styles that optimize land use.

Here are the various options worth considering.

1: Garden style apartment complexes: multi-family design

The first thing you need to keep in mind is that single-family developments are off the table. They are too risky and not an ideal fit for a scenario where land is a scarce commodity. If the goal is to maximize land-use without entering the luxury real estate segment, multi-family designs should be the norm, not the exception.

When it comes to multi-family designs, there are a number of them to go around, but for this book, we shall talk about the designs we have experienced much success at MarketSpace Capital.

Wrap building

Another name for this design would be the "Texas Donut," and the name is a proper fit because the design looks donut-shaped, or rather, the design takes the form of a multi-story building built around a centrally placed parking garage.

This design is not new; it has been around for more than a century, and has only undergone a few minor revisions throughout this period. It recently became even more popular in 2010, after modification made to the International Building Code to allow only a maximum construction of five stories with wood frames.

Nevertheless, it is one of the best to consider because it is a high-density solution that also happens to be relatively inexpensive to build. For instance, a density of 50 to 60 units per acre is highly achievable with this design.

When it comes to the cost, the results are even more impressive. In coastal California, which also happens to be one of the most expensive markets, construction with this design can go for anywhere between $175 and $225 for every rentable square foot.

This design also lends itself well to other cost-saving features like using pre-fabricated steel, which has proven to cut down construction time and needed space.

MarketSpace Capital is using this wrap concept in the Spot at Anderson (Houston) and the Spot at Myra Park (Dallas). These are perfect examples that demonstrate how well we have used this design to our advantage.

Let's now talk about the good and the bad associated with this design.

The pros

- The first obvious advantage is that they cost less to construct. Using wood-frames instead of steel and concrete means you are looking at a cheaper project overall.

- The second advantage is these buildings are likely very profitable because the design accommodates a high density. As mentioned, 50 to 60 units per acre is the norm. With a density like that, you are looking at a high return on investment.

- They allow for walkable streets. Since such structures are common in urban and suburban environments, their presence must not deprive residents of their desire to have comfortable and walkable streets which are ideal for strolls.

- They allow for municipal parking requirements.

The cons

- The first problematic aspect is the design is commonplace and trite. It looks manufactured, and seems to lack individuality because there is little room for creativity. This means the design is not very likely to impress the eyes unless the building is new.

- Another downside is this design requires a huge tract of land. It is typical for this architecture to sit on a 2-acre site. In a developed urban or suburban setting, land doesn't come easy or cheap. Thus, it sets a very high barrier for entry for someone who's undercapitalized.

2: Garden style apartment complexes

Next in line are the Garden Style apartment complexes. By definition, this design consists of residential units typically located at ground level, providing access to a lawn or garden space. Green spaces are not very popular in urban areas, making this design a better fit for semi-rural and suburban environments. It is also worth noting that apartment complexes that use this design never exceed three stories.

There're variations to this design, like the walk-up apartment featuring an outdoor staircase, and located on top of a parking garage with a parking lot option. In other instances, the apartment may be on the basement level. Whatever the case, the greens outside the units typify all garden-style apartments.

The advantages and disadvantages associated with this design include:

<u>The pros</u>

- The building has easy access, and the available, well-designated parking means that the tenant does not have to go through a lot of trouble to enter or leave the building.

- The green environment around the property gives it a luxurious look and feel, making the property desirable and rare for many urban and suburban dwellers. That means there is likely to be high competition among prospective tenants.

- The design is usually a better fit for spread-out neighborhoods free from the presence of mid to high-rise establishments. Such areas seem more luxurious, and such properties fetch a good price or rent.

<u>The cons</u>

- Land in lush and leafy suburbs tends to be very expensive to acquire, and at times the price may not justify the returns.

- Sometimes, the views associated with this type of property may not be ideal, decreasing desirability.

- Generally, garden-style apartments appreciate slower.

3: Co-living spaces in the sharing economy

Next is the concept of co-living spaces, which refers to the practice of two or more unrelated people sharing the same living space.

Although this design reflects a recent trend in architecture, the underlying idea is not at all new. Here's what I mean.

You are probably familiar with the idea of having a roommate. Maybe you had one when you were in college or you likely know someone who had one. Perhaps you had one when you first moved into the city to bring down rental costs. You also may have wanted human contact to help alleviate boredom.

The same concept applies to co-living space design. The idea is to approach the design with the concept of sharing resources among people. For instance, an architect may design a unit to code to ensure occupants have personal bathrooms, but they share the kitchen and the living room.

This idea is becoming more popular mainly because today, we live in a sharing economy. A sharing economy is a model that involves one person taking his or her asset and lending it to another who may want to use it on a short-term basis. The lender gets to earn some passive income from doing so. The cost-effectiveness afforded by this model is what makes it very attractive.

That said, let's talk about the pros and cons.

Today, with many young people getting attracted to the urban lifestyle and its profound economic consequences, a considerable number of them will be looking to cut costs in any way that they can.

One of the key cost-cutting areas is usually housing, which is part of the reason why this design is likely to do so well in the years to come.

The pros

- The design promotes a sense of community, something lacking in a typical urban lifestyle. That is part of this design's appeal; it helps people come together and escape the proverbial city loneliness.

- The cost-sharing nature inherent to this design lends itself well to the high living cost that typifies urban lifestyles. That means there will always be tenants appreciating its usefulness.

- This property's design is great for the ever-increasing number of traveling business people and digital nomads today, especially in many urban and suburban environments. Thus, the demand for this property is high, a trend that is likely to hold up.

The Cons

- This design concept is new, meaning it needs more time to prove itself. You might feel somewhat reserved about pursuing it because the concept doesn't have sufficient testing yet.

- There can be privacy concerns, making this property the kind that people lease for only a short period, leading to unpredictable cash flows.

Let's now move on and talk about current and future technology trends that will affect commercial real estate.

How the "15-Minute City" Will Change the World

As you look back in time, urban sprawl in the United States had its origins in the flight to the suburbs that began in the 1950s, and has accelerated with each decade. As suburban areas developed, cities expanded in geographic size faster than they grew in population. This trend has produced large metropolitan areas with low population densities, interconnected by roads, mass transit and other transportation arterials. But what does this urban sprawl mean for the traditional inner-city of America? Is the traditional city officially dead? And equally important is a contemporary question: Have the effects of the COVID-19 pandemic—with the elimination of community gathering places such as restaurants, bars, places of worship, parks and even offices—altered the shape, design, and characteristics of the traditional city?

These questions, as well as the conversations that have occurred over the past couple months, has caused urban planners to reevaluate the future of some of the most vibrant, energetic and powerful cities across America. In fact, a dichotomy exists. Many professionals have announced the death of modern cities, while others have not been so drastic and see change as a good thing for the citizenry of these major cities. After all, "The secret of change is to focus all of your energy not on fighting the old, but on building the new."

While these conversations have accelerated due to the coronavirus pandemic, there is more than one reason for things to change.

Whether it be health, environmental, or societal change, the "15-Minute City" is the way of the future.

What is the 15-Minute City?

The "15-Minute City" idea is based on research into how city dwellers' use of time could be reorganized to improve both living conditions and the environment. Developed by Professor Carlos Moreno at the Sorbonne in Paris, the concept of "la ville du quart d'heure" is one in which daily urban necessities are within a 15-minute reach on foot or by bike. Hence the name "15-Minute City." In short, work, home, shops, entertainment, education, and healthcare would all be available within the same time that a commuter might once have waited on a railway platform.

Within the 15-Minute City, the accent shifts from urban sprawl and territorial mobility to close and easy access. The strategy no longer focuses on pouring more and more concrete and opening roads more efficiently, but quite the opposite, by reducing displacements. Ideally, in a 15-Minute City, long-distance mobility is significantly reduced, and residents no longer depend on their private vehicles or public transportation for daily commuting.

In the 15-Minute City, the streetscape becomes the spine of the community. It is the community's core, the gathering place, the center of outdoor activities, a park and green space of sorts. Rescued from intense vehicle traffic, the streets come to life and become livable. These publicly-owned and maintained pieces of concrete and asphalt welcome and invite children's playgrounds, terraces, street art displays and shows, thereby increasing synergy and integration of the community. Put another way, this "urban space of excellence starts to reclaim its humanity."

While the 15 Minute City has a new shiny name, it is just a step into the past; a time before people commuted up to an hour into a business center to work.

Where Does it Fit Into the "New Normal?"

While this "urban evolution" was not initially intended to help with coronavirus protocols and stay-at-home mandates, it has fallen into its new role perfectly. With a pandemic and the resulting federal, state, and local requirements that necessitate people staying in or close to home, a city plan that allows for all necessities to be reached within a short distance walk is ideal. The COVID-19 pandemic has made us call into question ways in which we can improve on the idea of cities and city spaces. Cities have been hit hard by the pandemic. People have talked about a "new normal" that has been thrust upon us all. This new normal involves less travel, smaller circles and more space. These are all things that the 15-Minute City promotes.

Travel has been curtailed because of the coronavirus, and transportation may be changed forever. While the 15-Minute City cannot deal with air travel and other long-commute problems, it can greatly reduce everyday travel and short-run commutes. One of the ideas of the 15-Minute City is to make it possible to work, live, play, recreate, worship, etc. all in the same area where they live. Contrast that with a 30-minute to 1-hour drive to a city's central business district. This, and the effects of hindsight being 20-20 when it comes to the pandemic, would help slow the spread of the pandemic by lowering the number on new interactions with people, along with less exposure to large numbers of people.

Working conditions made an abrupt shift during 2020. While most jobs were previously performed in an office environment, an entire work force was forced to work from home as a safety measure to counteract COVID-19. This seemed like an easy and understandable solution, but it had some consequences.

There are many people who do not have the space or resources to work from home. Some people simply do not have the luxury of a spare room to set up an in-home office. Some do not have family nearby to help with childcare, as schools were also shut down. Some do not have reliable internet connection. Unfortunately, there are certain factors to working from home that disenfranchise everyone's lifestyle, especially lower income people. While people transition away from big offices in the city, small offices in the 15-Minute City is a good solution.

Everyone has heard of the "New Normal" and what that might entail. Many people will never see this new form of living as an upgrade or an improvement to their lives; it seems like a world of less freedom, less interaction, and less gatherings. Yet, indoctrinating the 15-Minute City as the new normal can be easy, and actually very beneficial to those who are accepting of the new urban design characteristics. In fact, people will save money, be healthier, be more productive, and rekindle a sense of community within their neighborhoods. While a post COVID-19 world has many uncertainties, a world with a 15-Minute City may be a strong antidote.

Environment

While it has not been the lead story in every newspaper during the past four-year administration, environmental concerns are ubiquitous and are not going away. Unfortunately, in the past few decades the myriad of approaches on how to manage the environment has become very politicized. However, everybody wants cleaner water, soil, and air. In short, everyone wants a cleaner world. Most of the arguments that moderate people have made evolve around the fiscal impact and the logistics related to its implementation. The 15-Minute City was designed with the very purpose of healing the environment, and in addition to alternative fuels, would be a great way to help clean the earth. As workplaces, stores, and homes are brought into closer proximity, street space previously dedicated to auto congestion is freed up, thereby eliminating pollution, and making way for gardens, hike and bike lanes, sports and leisure facilities.

In current city planning, it is almost certain that most US citizens have to get in a car to get groceries, go to a restaurant, bar, movie, doctor's appointment, grocery store, place of worship, etc. With the 15-Minute City, towns will become more sustainable, as less car travel will be necessary.

Eight-five percent of Americans commute to work, and many of those travel between 30-minutes and one hour. This is a major problem for many environmental, societal, economic, and efficiency reasons, yet this is where an opportunity opens up for the 15-Minute City to work its magic. With the COVID effect causing most people in America to work from home, many companies have learned they do not really need the expensive downtown offices anymore. Some, like British Petroleum, have decided to completely switch to remote working throughout London, while others have the plan to reopen but with mini offices located in these 15-Minute City environments. Both strategies are helpful to the environment as a whole, and could remove so much unnecessary added carbon to the atmosphere.

Overall, the 15-Minute City will help the climate as it was designed by urban planners with that goal in mind. When it comes to environmental protection, many get hung up on the fiscal costs, subsidies, and required investments. But the 15-Minute City is a "supply-side" economic benefit as it saves the ultimate taxpayer money in the process. With the 15-Minute City, streets can see a major decline in automobiles and fuel consumption, thereby reducing CO_2 emissions. With the alternative land use and increase of garden and green space, the resulting photosynthesis increases oxygen production. The net result of all these factors is that we have both a cleaner environment, as well as an economic stimulus package due to the supply side economic benefits and a more efficient work force. Who could ask for more?

How Does This Effect the Community?

Ever since the exponential rise in population and the effects of urban sprawl on big cities, we have slowly lost our sense of a community. We are no longer in Maybury RFD or Utopia where people would bond with a common interest over a community goal, mission, or project within their locale. Sometimes chaos and crisis bring a community together. Yet as we have seen this year, chaos has brought greater separation. Due to the pandemic induced isolation, people have only been able to communicate remotely, and have had a lot of time on their hands to let social media accelerate a divisive wedge during a highly contested election cycle.

The 15-Minute City calls for a return to a more local community, with a somewhat slower way of life, where commuting time is instead invested in richer relationships with those nearby. The urban planners are hopeful that the smaller geographic footprint, and the closeness that accompanies the 15-Minute City, might also bring back a since of civility that is so desperately needed. The COVID crisis show us the possibility for rediscovering proximity. Now, more than ever, we as people, need proximity. Not because of the potential vaccine, the environment, or any other issue, but for the act of human interaction and the overall humanizing of one another.

In today's master-planned, spacious society, you would be lucky to know more than a couple of your neighbors. People are so fixated on their day-to-day lives, and do not really know who lives around them anymore. The world is too fast paced for things like a neighborhood cocktail or block party. What the 15-Minute City brings to the world is a return to simplicity. We have lost sight of what it means to be a neighbor and part of a community. It will allow us to slow down, no longer rushing to work or the doctor's office, but maybe a nice walk or bike ride to simply get groceries.

Innovation Through Regression

The idea for the 15-Minute City is nothing new. In fact, in America it began with the first Settlers on Plymouth Rock and has been replicated repeatedly, from community to community. Now it has been repackaged, branded under a new name, and is being marketed as the 15-Minute City. Same strategy and goal, yet with a new fancy name.

If you went "Back to the Future" in almost any era of US history, you would see that most communities had a "live, work, play, shop, learn, worship, recreate, etc." environment in a close-knit community. Yes, transportation may have been by foot, horse, train, Model T, or mass transit, but the effects of urban sprawl truly changed these communities—as well as society—and the effects of this change has been very far reaching.

With the 15-Minute City, we bring back some of the old ideas to revitalize our communities, improve the environment, enhance our productivity, and heal our society. After all, "the secret of change is to focus all of your energy not on fighting the old, but on building the new." While we always look for the next big thing for the future, it is sometimes best to look in the past at an idea that we left behind a long time ago.

NOTES

Name_____

Address_____

℞ CHAPTER EIGHT

CURRENT AND FUTURE TECHNOLOGY TRENDS

Refills_____

M.D _____

"Real estate is an imperishable asset, ever-increasing in value. It is the most solid security that human ingenuity has devised. It is the basis of all security and about the only indestructible security."
Russell Sage, American financier, and politician

"My largest business accomplishment was forming MarketSpace Capital to handle all of my real estate needs. The story is ongoing, and even though we all gauge success in different ways, by every metric I am pleased with the results thus far. From a motivation standpoint, the biggest factor in my life was my Asian mom. Yes, she drove me nuts sometimes, but she made sure that I gave 110 percent at everything—or otherwise face dire consequences. This habit of giving it your all becomes engrained in your DNA and becomes the way of approaching everything in life."
Dr. Masaki Oishi, Real Estate Investor

Unless you have been living under a rock for the past few decades, you are acutely aware of how heavily technology has influenced the modern world. Indeed, human beings have come a long way.

Today, we see technology-driven changes considered impossible by society. Back in the early 2000s, could you imagine issuing voice commands to Alexa? I know, neither did I.

Despite all the technological revolution, many people perceive real estate as being somewhat resistant to technological influence. Even today, many things in real estate are still "old school." However, that reality is slowly changing. Technology has managed to make its way into real estate, and the predictable ramifications are likely to be profound, if not downright disruptive.

This chapter will introduce you to some ways that technology keeps impacting real estate investment so that you can prepare accordingly for them.

PropTech

Proptech is a new word that describes the use of technology in real estate. Any use of technology in traditional real estate procedures, such as property acquisition, due diligence, management, transaction processes, investment, and so on, all fall under PropTech.

Big Data

Big Data relates to how large amounts of data impact a business's daily operation. It has the characteristic of being both structured and unstructured and cannot be analyzed using traditional means.

Big Data has profound implications in Real Estate because most sound business decisions are data-based. Therefore, Big Data will revolutionize what has always worked best, thereby making it better.

Companies like Zillow, Redfin, Trulia, and others are already using Big Data. Effectively, what these firms are doing is using

Big Data technology to scrap information and collect and analyze massive amounts of data regarding area traffic, consumer surveys, demographic information, buying and selling trends, and more. This type of analysis puts these companies in a better position to provide valuable and actionable insights on the potential value of homes, supply and demand patterns, pricing, and so on.

Property managers and current owners also benefit from this Big Data technology. Real-time and historical maintenance information can now be made available through devices such as electrical appliances, HVAC systems, fire and safety systems, utilities, and more.

Using Big Data technology, potential problems in properties can be identified in real-time or even beforehand and rectified. Thus, productivity and quality of service improve overall.

Artificial Intelligence (AI) and Machine Learning

Artificial Intelligence and Machine Learning will serve to make the data amassed in real estate more actionable. For instance, consider property searches on websites like Zillow.com. Presently, searching involves using definite parameters such as an address, neighborhood, city or zip code. It's a pretty static and monotonous process.

In the future, artificial intelligence and machine learning algorithms will revolutionize the search process and make it more dynamic and fun. The process will be more personalized to suit individual tastes and preferences.

How would you like to arrive at a site that recognizes several basic things about you before you begin the search process? Even better, how would you like to conduct the process via voice commands?

Such is what is achievable with AI and Machine Learning algorithms. Want an example? Look at how advanced Google search has become today and compare it with what it used to be only a few years ago.

Another up-and-coming area of real estate that AI and Machine Learning algorithms will redefine is agent and customer support. These days, we increasingly see the use of chatbots in providing answers to basic customer queries. Given the right questions, bots can answer some pretty standard queries, which is great all by itself.

However, the exciting thing about chatbots is they thrive on the backbone of artificial intelligence and machine learning algorithms. That means they get smarter as they interact with people and receive more data from developers. Essentially, they can learn both from the data they receive and from the operations they complete.

Pretty soon, we can expect chatbots to be pretty self-sufficient and almost as smart as human beings. They can help cut down expenses on support staff, agent fees, and provide round-the-clock support. That is mesmerizing.

Virtual and Augmented Reality

Virtual and Augmented reality will also likely affect real estate in many different ways.

First, it can help agents sell to prospects who are far away by offering them virtual property tours from wherever they are. That is an enhanced experience, especially considering that 50 percent of real estate buyers first conduct their research online before showing up in person for a tour.

Second, it can help with the staging process. Usually, real estate companies spend fortunes on furnishings meant to improve the emotional appeal that pushes buyers into committing to a purchase.

With virtual reality, furniture and other equipment can be digitally placed and presented to the prospect at a steep discount in cost. Such savings on cost can boost investor performance significantly.

Third, this technology can also make significant contributions to architecture. As of now, most architects present their projects via drawings on paper and miniature models. VR and AR technology could make things better by allowing for more realistic presentations that involve 3D cinematic demonstrations. That could enhance the viewer experience and helps them get a feel of what they are paying for and the final product.

Virtual tours will also benefit property managers tasked with finding new tenant replacements and getting them acquainted with the property's facilities. Virtual Reality will help enhance that process without involving many hassles and time wastage.

Internet of Things (IoT)

IoT is a term that refers to the class of gadgets and devices that have network connectivity and that constantly send and receive performance data and other information relating to their daily use.

You can consider IoT devices to be smart devices. For instance, consider a washing machine that is controllable by and that relays status information on a tablet or mobile phone. Such devices could also relay critical performance data to technical support teams who will keep a close eye on metrics that will likely indicate trouble and show up to rectify the problem before it gets out of hand. This will result in reduced maintenance costs for property owners and enhanced user experience for the tenants.

Experts envision even more large-scale implementations of IoT in the future. Think of how the concept of smart cities that relay real-time information would play out. All the while, Big Data technologies are sifting through the data, using it to provide all sorts of insights and useful recommendations for further actions.

5G

5G represents internet connectivity that provides higher bandwidth; bandwidth is a technical term for the data transfer rate.

A high bandwidth connection implies a faster data transference rate and more reliably. That can make a huge difference, especially in situations where reliability could make a difference. Take the issue of security, for instance.

Today, security cameras and other home security appliances are IoT devices-equipped with internet connectivity. For example, alarm triggers get sent out throughout the internet to ensure they reach relevant parties on time for appropriate action.

A high bandwidth connection is necessary for such devices to be relevant. Unfortunately, our present 4G connectivity may suffer bottlenecks that affect the reliability of such systems. 5G promises even better.

Drones

The importance of drone technology in real estate cannot go unmentioned. One of the most significant contributions drones have had so far is helping produce breathtaking aerial views of property at a cost-friendly price. Previously, such productions would have cost many thousands of dollars and would at times eat into the profit generated from a sale.

Another real possibility presented by drones is providing real-time property tours from a remote location. Using 5G technology, it's possible to safely fly drones equipped with cameras that relay high-definition camera footage to the prospective buyer or tenants into properties.

Such remote site visits can also help prospects pinpoint possible issues with a property that could help with the negotiation process.

Building Information Modeling (BIM)

BIM refers to technology that renders three-dimensional images of architectural plans. It has the potential to transform traditional hand-drawn sketches into complex 3D models. It should be evident to anyone that 3D models are easier to interpret and apply than 2-dimensional pictorial representations and drawings.

That is a real breakthrough for the people who must use these sorts of plans, such as architects, construction professionals, and engineers.

Through this technology, the process of planning, designing, constructing, even managing buildings and infrastructure has transformed into something better.

Geolocation

Geolocation technology can transform simple maps into data presentation charts. It enables real estate experts to visualize critical data on a location-by-location basis. For instance, you can determine buying or selling strength in a particular location. You can also get a sense of the actual population data, demographics, actual sales price of properties in the areas, and much more. That can be very instrumental because it helps with the analysis process.

For example, property valuations can be more accurate. Land use planning and risk-reward analysis become easier. Even marketing property takes on a new dimension.

GeothinQ is one company that is providing access to such technology to real estate market participants on demand.

Blockchain

Blockchain is the technology behind popular cryptocurrencies such as Bitcoin, Ethereum, and others. Ever since cryptocurrencies became popular, many have stripped down and studied the technology at the molecular level, revealing important discoveries.

As it turns out, the technology is robust and could have diverse, remarkable applications. One such area is commerce, and real estate title certainly happens to be one of the fortunate areas that could benefit immensely.

You see, real estate is a market that suffers from various shortcomings. These include:

- A lack of transparency regarding price, ownership and transaction history
- A lack of liquidity
- A high barrier to entry due to price

- High transaction costs

These are all problem areas that Blockchain technology could fix. Here are some of the ways.

#1: Blockchain will introduce transparency in real estate

Let's look at the first case involving a lack of transparency.

In real estate, determining the right price is highly subjective because people do not use the same data. Also, ownership documents are still paper-based in many nations, making them easy to forge, manipulate or just plain destroy.

Even more concerning is the fact that transaction history is not easily trackable. That makes this market a perfect playground for criminals looking to launder money. Often, wealth from unknown origin finds itself in these markets simply because of a lack of transparency. Estimates indicate that approximately 30 percent of the money in real estate has criminal origins.

These are all problems that blockchain technology could solve. For one thing, blockchain technology has the characteristics of decentralization and immutability.

By decentralized, we mean information stored in the network is viewable by everyone. Thus, the issue of shrouding ownership information, price, and transaction history in secrecy quickly go out the window.

Immutability refers to any one person's inability to tamper with the integrity of the data stored. Thus, the idea of falsifying ownership information, manipulating price data or transaction records also gets quickly dismissed.

Therefore, because of these small changes alone, transparency gets introduced into the marketplace, making playing this market a lot safer.

#2: Blockchain will improve liquidity and reduce the barrier to entry

Next, we move to the issue of liquidity. In real estate, transactions often involve large amounts of money that many people do not have access to, creating a big barrier to entry for people of smaller means.

This is a problem for current participants because the lack of liquidity also means that transactions often cannot take place in a short amount of time without affecting price. Real estate transactions often have to take place at below market value, and when someone is in a hurry, the price decreases further.

Blockchain technology offers the ability to tokenize tradable instruments. By tokenization, we mean splitting asset ownership into small parts. Thus, someone can own a fractional share of a piece of property.

The obvious advantage here is that ordinary, less-capitalized people can suddenly become market participants since fractional shares are cheaper to own than an entire block. In other words, tokenization makes possible it possible to securitize real estate like any other financial instrument out there.

Consequently, the real estate market will become much more liquid because ownership is available to a much larger audience. Therefore, short-term price gyrations caused by participants entering and exiting the market participants will virtually cease to be a problem.

#3: Blockchain will reduce transaction costs

Last, there is the problem of transaction costs, which are very high in real estate because of the middle-men who perform standard procedures and who get compensated for their efforts.

The irony of it all is that these professional tasks are virtually eliminated or standardized in other liquid markets. For instance, in the stock market, the broker only offers access to the market, and transaction costs are significantly low.

There is also no need for an appraiser because everybody knows the price. Additionally, inspectors aren't unnecessary because, by law, all information about the stock should be public knowledge. Anyone can perform a personal analysis or hire an analyst if they wish to.

There is no need to draft paperwork every time, or involve lawyers, because all transactions have easy-to-trace electronic standardization. You could be an owner of a Microsoft stock this morning and transfer ownership rights to someone else by afternoon.

Blockchain's decentralized and immutability nature means that transactions can take place with virtually the same level of efficiency and transparency as in the stock market, thereby eliminating countless intermediaries, making transaction costs cheaper.

Blockchain technology has a lot of promise for real estate and could be a real game-changer. It helps to keep a close eye on its impact because it could soon transform the game as we know it; you never want to get caught on the wrong side of such a transformation.

Name_____

Address _____

R℣ CONCLUSION

Refills_____

M.D _____

We have now come to the end of our sojourn together. I want to thank you and congratulate you for having the patience and discipline to stick with me to the end.

In this book, we have exhaustively looked at several things related to investing in real estate. We have talked about topics ranging from:

- Why real estate is a good investment
- To the myths
- To the risks
- To the factors affecting real estate
- To how to conduct due diligence
- To a formulaic approach to selecting appropriate property investments
- To transaction structuring

- To the various technologies affecting real estate

Without a doubt, the journey has been long, but you made it. You can now rest assured that you know more than most medical professionals—or professionals in other fields—will ever know about real estate.

With the knowledge you now have, it is less risky for you than it will be for anyone who knows close to nothing. You can go forward and conquer real estate investing, knowing that you are not operating blindly and without an idea of what you are doing.

Remember, you do not have to keep working hard, paying huge taxes, and letting what you have left sitting in the bank doing nothing. That is a risky way of operating that could set you back financially in a few decades to come.

It is a lot safer to park your money in a place where it will earn a decent return and even allow you to build wealth slowly and retire rich. If you diligently apply the knowledge you have learned from this book, you could one day retire with a seven or eight-figure net worth, or perhaps more. Who in the world would not want a luxury like that?

The choice is yours. Only you can decide what to do with the knowledge you now have.

As I have "prescribed" many times in the past, if you have decided to take the passive route to real estate investing, I invite you to join me at MarketSpace Capital.

At MarketSpace Capital, you will share my passion and vision for real estate, an asset I became familiar with when I was a 15 year-old boy. We will take you through everything we have in this book discussed so far, plus a lot more.

By the end of our meeting, you will feel that the money you have worked so hard for could never be in safer hands. You will also know that it will keep working as hard as you do, day and night, so that one day you can retire with the wealth and freedom you've always desired.

I hope that the time you have spent reading this book has been of value to you, and I truly hope to meet you in the future!

All the best in your real estate investing!

Dr. Masaki Oishi

Notes